HOW TO CHEAT ON YOUR HUSBAND AND NEVER GET CAUGHT

Defying the Double Standard

By

Bunny Wingate

Illustrations by Polly Coté

First published by AuthorHouse 03/10/05

ISBN: 1-4184-7077-5 (e-book)
ISBN: 1-4184-5348-X (Paperback)

Printed in the United States of America
Bloomington, Indiana

This book is printed on acid free paper.

This book never would have been written if all the Tom's Joey's and Andre's in my life had been all the fools I and so many other women have suffered. There would not have been a need to instruct so in the art of Cheating for such men are to be cherished and held high in great esteem as they are the best of men.

They know who they are and I thank them for loving me as a woman and as a friend when I needed to be held and caressed with great passion and kind intimacy. So much to be learned from such men, so much to be learned from me.

To Anthony... You have my heart.

Foreword

Many of you married women read how-to books and articles on sensuality. There is *Everything You Always Wanted To Know About Sex But Were Afraid to Ask*, the birds and the bees with blazing, full-color illustrations and three hundred erotic positions. Also available: how to seduce Mafia chieftains and other average guys, and lots of general knowledge on what to do with your hair, wardrobe, flabby body and furniture once the action begins. You possess all the information you need, except that no one, until now, ever defined in detail how to enjoy all this wild abandon without getting caught.

The liberated woman always lives in another neighborhood while we vicariously live through her experiences in Cosmo and Playgirl. We may have come a long way, baby, with cigarettes and funky clothes, but many of us still struggle with morality taboos and frustrated fantasies from years gone by. This stems from a fear of losing the lives we built scrubbing diapers, and a lack of precedents to show us the way. Few women, unless they enjoy living on the brink of disaster, share their step-by-step journey into infidelity with their female friends. If they do talk, don't take their advice. They violate the cardinal rule of cheating—secrecy.

Honor among thieves and the promiscuous exists mainly in the male domain. Rarely will a man rat on his friend. He offers his apartment, car, office, and sometimes even his bed partner to a fellow philanderer. Men form a strong fraternity of tradition, and if one of their comrades needs help they lie singularly or in groups to save him. I know of no sorority that attempts the same.

We must also deal with the double standard. Even with all the liberating under way, a Don Juan lady only looks good in a magazine layout. In real life, her female counterparts often look upon her as the PTA slut. Some men now accept the female desire for occasional polygamous pursuits as natural and desirous—as long as it isn't their wives polygamizing. Some men accept the changing role of the woman more quickly than the women who picket and scream for it. That's why I'm writing this book. These men, while waiting for you to live out your fantasies, will not judge you. They anticipate the gifts you possess, and treat you with respect, frankness and honesty. Those unable to handle it will be discussed in future chapters.

I am a divorced woman with two children. Had I relied on one man to fulfill all of my needs, I would now be a dependent, nagging shrew totally consumed by delusions about my life if I had ignored my needs when they presented themselves. I made horrendous mistakes at the beginning of my voyage, but luck and the ability to keep my wits saved me when the luck ran out. You can benefit from my mistakes as well as my triumphs. Some rare, warm relationships benefited everyone, including my husband, who came home to a smiling wife with a martini on ice. This book was written with husbands one and two in mind. My present lover is a jewel among men. A ruby in a sea of diamonique. Faithful for me is required with such a man.

A successful seduction requires maturity, a trait many women lack. If screwing the world haphazardly turns you on, this is not the book for you. I'm not putting down sporty one-nighters if the mood strikes you. It's haphazard deviltry I can't condone. Sure, swiveling wildly on a strange penis can excite, as long as you take the necessary precautions. But this book advocates discreet, planned action. If wrecking your marriage motivates you, find less painful ways to do it.

A growing army of married women in this great nation of ours wants two cars in every garage, two chickens in every pot, and two men in separate beds. If this includes you, keep reading for tips on achieving the latter with as little difficulty and as much fun as possible.

"There's the husband who treats his wife like a teething infant."

CHAPTER 1
Why Do We Cheat?

Before we explore not getting caught, let's briefly examine the reasons and the needs for cheating. I say "cheating" because most men and women use the word for this social pastime. If, in your case, the mental commitment in marriage no longer exists and you're staying together for all the wrong reasons, cheating is the wrong word. Your marriage ended a long time ago, but for some reason you want to maintain the lie. You live together basically as roommates with very little else. You can't cheat on nothing. I will continue using the word, even for you, to avoid confusion. Try to know your reason. It will help in choosing the right man to compensate for the holes in your life.

The main reasons we cheat include:

Boredom. This rates as the chief cause, based on the comments of more than six hundred women I quizzed. It's a rare marriage where both parties maintain the mystique over a number of years. Marriage is hard work, and most of us are too tired from competing in the daily rat race to hold a night job as well. I know couples who are fascinating as individuals but dull in tandem. Boredom does not necessarily equal a bad marriage. Warmth, friendship and memories with a truly nice man may be too precious to discard. If you can tolerate nocturnal yawning and fill your days with interesting hobbies, you're to be envied. If the boredom becomes a major source of irritation, consider scratching your scuba diving class in favor of something less liquid and more solid.

If the boredom connects with an insensitive, loutish, prefrontal-lobotomy sitting at the dinner table, I would have to hold a mirror to your mouth hoping to see a fog if you didn't hit the Sleepy Hollow Hotel at least once a week. True, many women can survive and even ignore the comatose body that crawls into the driveway promptly at six p.m. If you're in this group, return this book or lend it to a friend in need. Before doing this, I recommend you read it in plain view of the stiff when he's inhaling his cookies and milk. You may as well get your money's worth in shock value if nothing else.

Curiosity. You married at a tender age, caught up in the frenzy of your girlfriends waving their one-carat rocks in Sociology 202. Now most of these vestal virgins' rocks are hot. Can being with only one man for life be so terrible? Men all possess the same equipment, albeit in different sizes, and you always knew that it's not the quantity but the quality that counts; right? You feel sexually fulfilled, but, once before you die, you'd like to make sure you're not missing something. If you find out what's missing, however, do not become the happy hooker with hubby overnight unless you're enrolled in a sex education class at a reputable university. Find a subtle way to introduce the new techniques. If he's dense or a creature of habit, forget it like the aftermath of a final exam. You can continue your quest for knowledge with a variety of tutors. This can get tricky as you advance toward your doctorate while your husband remains stuck at the sixth grade level. Try keeping your eyes open during marital sex so you don't

3

forget who's on top, lest you thrash about in an unusual manner arousing *his* curiosity.

Piggish hedonism. You've got it all but want more. No one is making value judgments on these pages. We all experience different levels of satisfaction, and monogamy doesn't work for everyone. In any case, you have the most to lose, so I suggest you memorize this and all other material pertaining to fooling around.

You let yourself go for ten years. Suddenly you find strength and pull it all together. Compliments roll in from everyone, including the kids' guitar teacher, who plucks a mean string. Every time you look in the mirror, it's such a pleasant change from last year's dry heaves. Your weight is down and your hormones are up. Propositions pour in. (Even if it's only one, consider it a pour.) Remember the retching sounds from the family physician as you disrobed for your annual physical? How many years did you live with "Such a pretty face and terrific personality; if only you could drop fifty pounds."

A star is born. Remain outwardly modest even as your ego expands. Sooner or later, everyone will become used to the new body and start picking on some other imperfection. So, before your comet falls to earth, the ten years you wasted as a fatty must be made up in ten days, remembering, however, that the risk factor for impetuous, indiscriminate screwing is high. If you look good now, you'll look just as good next month; probably better as you make more improvements. Hold off. Live with the body and learn control techniques.

The urge to throw it all over town will be overwhelming but unwise. If possible, make do with your husband, whatever he is. I have encountered cases of ex-tubbies who turned their husbands on so much they didn't need outside-the-home sex. Some felt satiated by the extra attention; others pooped out for the same reason.

Revenge. This emotion arises from all sorts of experiences. You hate him for turning you into a professional laundry and dry cleaning service. Before your marriage, you modeled clothes; now you scrub them.

The lumbering oaf, thinking you a fool, gets caught in the sack with a girl. He rushed into the affair so rapidly even an Inspector Clouseau could have caught him, plus he has the affrontery to sleep with a dog. The ultimate put-down. He takes the path of least resistance because the sleaze cares not a whit for your feelings. He adds salt to the wound by making your friends wonder what *your* problem is because he gets off, another primarily male phrase, with a lady who looks like she dines on kibble.

It's possible that your revenge is as simple as he is. He could be a nuclear physicist or a plumber, either one of which takes some thought and skill. But when he comes home, he reverts to a brainless clod completely indifferent to your feelings. You're not even asking for remembrances of birthdays or anniversaries, although that would be nice. All you ask is some semblance of a husband who is still paper-trained. Whether these passive ploddings come from a dulled brain or simple thoughtlessness, they remain intolerable.

Being taken for granted. Some of us will try any trick to be noticed short of draping ourselves nude around the office Sparkletts container during his coffee break. The dew is off the rose after many years of marriage. You're fed up with your status as a piece of nothing. Whatever good you enjoyed in the beginning is worth fighting for. A knock-down, drag-out brawl would be a welcome change from the zombie-like state of the union now. When he yawns at the peek-a-boo bra and black garterbelt, and ignores the spike heels attached to the mesh-hosed legs, it's time to pack up the underwear for a split week at the nearest motor lodge. Just make sure this kind of get-up doesn't attract a sex fiend equipped with chains. You tried extremes with a familiar man who looked through you. The new guy notices everything for the first time, and spike heels connote a certain kind of sexual preference on the first date. For safety's sake, try sporty tennis shoes.

Then there's the husband who treats his wife like a teething infant. The only thing he overlooks is taking her playpen to parties. He does allow her the monumental decisions of planning and cooking dinner and choosing the right wax to rub on *his* furniture. Beyond that, her thoughts are filed in the discard bin. He assures her that she definitely ranks one step above a dodo and she should be thankful for that. King Kong makes sure every day the occupants of his home know that his brilliance feeds and clothes them. Delegating any authority would surely doom the advancement of his career and family. This kind of treatment often sends his cooing, thumb-sucking baby into a strange crib where she slowly advances to the toddler stage and beyond with her own Dr. Spock.

Workaholicism. You're married to a work machine IBM computer. He channels all of his energies into his job. He makes you feel guilty if you disturb his productive years by asking for a double feature and a hamburger on Tuesday nights. He exacerbates matters if his important position is with the gas company reading meters. So, devoid of his presence, you also lack credit cards and new clothes. I find that the wives of successful executives survive longer with therapy provided at major department stores and boutiques. If you're waiting for the meter reader to become head gas man, don't shove your head in the oven; look for the discarded executive. It's easier suffering at Saks.

The wife beater. I only mention this callous brute to suggest the utmost caution. If he pummels you for burning his toast, imagine what would happen in a strange boudoir. The only good that could arise from his sudden raging burst into the room would be a manslaughter charge that puts him away for twenty years.

"The last call to supper." That's how Dr. David Reuben describes a syndrome affecting women when they approach the golden years, their children grown and enjoying a basically good marriage. Our youth-oriented society frightens this type of lady. Facing rough competition, she knows that if she doesn't score soon, the young stuff will devour all the available material. For decades men wailed the fifties blues while their wives sat patiently, waiting for them to come to their senses. Before achieving their geezerhood, they yearn for one last fling with their secretaries to prove they're not old and impotent. You may desire the same privilege. Well, you can't have it. I can't imagine a husband sitting by the tube understanding your fling with the kids' camp director as a desperate ego-soothing need. You're not allowed this psychological problem. If you want your "last call to supper" before the arthritis sets in, don't come crying to your nice husband to exorcise any guilt you feel. He'll deposit you in a home for the bewildered and dictate that his secretary sign the papers as a witness to your senility.

There aren't enough years to experience all that life offers. Your zest for living drives you, seeking a drink from every cup. You know who you are even if you pursue a zillion interests that don't match, and possess a genuine interest in the human race. Everything seems a glorious mystery with you as Sherlock Holmes trying to solve them all. You sublimate these yearnings for years, unaware of their existence because of your love for your husband. You felt them before you married, and it was only a matter of time before they surfaced again. As homo sapiens, we still remain part of the animal kingdom, incapable of going against our natural instincts. The stronger amongst you may fight the battle to your grave. Monogamy wins, but you pay a price for the victory. Someone said, "I'd rather be a live coward than a dead hero," about soldiers fighting in battle. Aren't we?

Few of us can stand the extremes, and yet we continue the marriage for financial security or dependency. Everyone has a breaking point. The weaker ones among us take longer to make the final break. Few of us can cut the string without bouncing on it for a while, hence cheating. My experience indicates that cheating on a really rotten marriage is a sheer waste of time. Why knock yourself out with fabrications with the end at hand? What good will it do anointing your ego in the afternoons if your louse, the spouse, beats you over the head every night? Flee the coop and start again.

If, on the other hand, the end seems far out of sight or invisible for whatever reasons, then take time out: chart a pleasant and intelligent course, hoping no one suffers. More positive even than that statement: hoping that at least one of you, if not both, benefits.

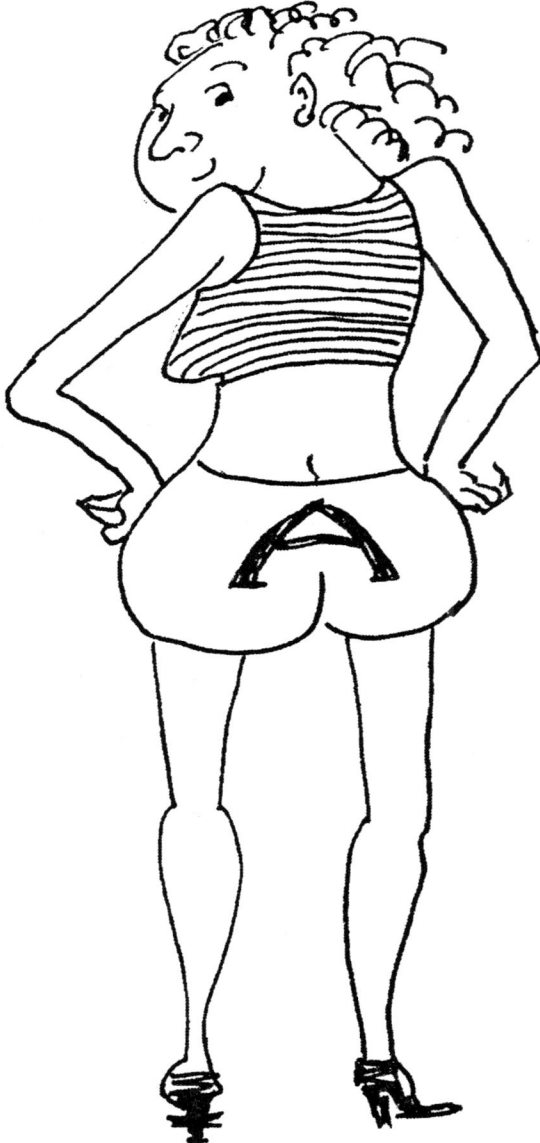

"Be the first female in your community sporting a scarlet letter on your hot pants."

CHAPTER 2

Open Marriage and Other Disasters

Along with the books on basic sex, we see all about us a more dangerous form of literature written by "experts." These godlike creatures of mind control—psychiatrists, psychologists and social science freaks—exert a frightening hold on the average and above-average seeker of truth. They dig into their statistics and concoct their idea of a panacea for the climbing divorce rate. If they actually lived the way they wrote for any length of time, their pain would make them retract every word of their bibles, I believe.

No one, even those with impressive titles, owns the right to extol the virtues of open marriage, swinging and sex clinics as an all-encompassing answer for everyone. I am not saying, "Cheat on your husband to secure a happy marriage." I merely offer advice based on my own experiences for ladies who choose this lifestyle so their marriages, some of them good, will not shoot down the tubes because the lady of the house requires a strange piece of tail (to coin a popular male locker room phrase).

Women are in mental transition now, confused by their natural biological urge toward polygamy that society has been squelching since the caveman clubbed his first inamorata. Suddenly, a good part of the world is lifting the ban on this urge, giving us the green light to fornicate at will. We are first-generation libbies, like babies attempting their first steps.

I have never been a faddist. My forays into infidelity were not dictated by the latest fad. I did what made me feel good in a sensible fashion before it became fashionable. Masses of fad followers now providing women with lip service actually fear admitting that their own personal feelings may not be in style. They scream, "do it, do it, do it," to your face, and whisper, "slut," "tramp" or "harlot," behind your back. Those who accept and admire the free female make no judgments, and usually represent a silent minority. Only time will tell if the present attitude toward polygamy becomes an open way of life. Until it happens, keep your mouth zipped at your luncheons and quilting bees unless your stamina qualifies you to be the first female in your community sporting a scarlet letter on your hot pants.

Open marriage is my first target. I know about open marriages that work when the contract for this kind of arrangement occurs at the outset of the union. It seems the most sensible approach for those of us who find monogamy an impossible way of life. Both partners must tune in on exactly the same wavelength, however, with enough maturity and control to forgo its use as a weapon in marital wars. Marriage presents enough problems with toothpaste tubes squeezed fore or aft and opposing views on the rearing of children without adding the extra burden of dealing with one's inadequacies when your spouse ranks the backup mate as momentarily perfect. If this double Mormon-like standard existed in our youth, open marriage, with all its faults and virtues, would prevail much like our present monogamous practice. We'd live in a giant *kibbutz* and the word "bastard" would never have been invented. As it stands now, the theory is radical and diametrically opposed to the feelings of jealousy.

A hundred years passed and countless race riots occurred before the black man made a small dent in his image and way of life. If it took this much social pressure for a ride on the same bus as a white man, how can an "expert" tell us, "run for the nearest strange bed after reading my book," with our spouse's blessings and approval? The twenty-first century human animal would need the mind control of an android adjusting to the quashing of his natural jealousy and monumental ego. The questions raised in the mind of the partner who receives this offer usually produce disastrous results.

A couple I know racked up a twenty-year traditional marriage with neither of the partners participating in extramarital sex. The husband then became an eager open marriage fan. He thought, "I'll do my wife a favor by not going elsewhere in secret." He proclaimed his honesty while beating his chest like the dumb ape he was. "Of course," he told her, "you're free to choose anyone you want." After living with the same woman for twenty years, you'd think he might have *some* inkling into her psyche. Whatever fears she harbored about her person or personality immediately surfaced. Following what she regarded as total rejection, she admitted experiencing polygamous thoughts for years. She became a whining, teary wreck even though he dropped the idea after her initial response. His definitive statement, with all its honesty and noble intent, shattered her ego. She wasn't good enough for him, etc. Ridiculous hypocrisy, yes, but the monogamous state of matrimony was the only state she knew. "If he'd cheated on me and I caught him, I could have forgiven his stupid mistake," she said. As ludicrous as it sounds, it's our right and wrong and the only game in town.

Swingers deal with essentially the same problems, but magnified a thousand times. They do their number together. They may occupy separate rooms or not, with four people or forty, heterosexual or homosexual, watching their mates with vivid fantasies of a slow, painful death, preferably before he or she reaches the big O.

My opinion of a couple's fornication is a strong DUMB. I am not condemning the common orgy. Orgiastic sex, which I participated in *before* marrying, proved gratifying, exciting and a terrific release from tensions and other afflictions of modern society. Love, respect and esteem rarely surface in group sex except for the fleeting feeling of gratitude one may experience for the penis that finally brings you to climax. Considering the typical crowded conditions and craziness of the moment, I often couldn't find, let alone thank, the owner of the satisfying organ. When I think of all the unthanked organs roaming the world, an overpowering sadness overwhelms me. So many great lays lost in the shuffle. Swinging does provide you with variety. This is the only positive statement I can make. On the negative side, I find degradation, jealousy, dehumanization, *ad infinitum*.

I have known many swinging marrieds. The most common problem? One partner usually attracts the best action, while the other half, who may be less attractive or sexually timid, is tolerated. To swing, you must come in twos, and it's difficult to find equally endowed twos. This creates insecurity, grudging pettiness and lots of glandular competition. The inequality of marriage, which couples can hide in the seclusion of the home, looms for all the world to see once the party begins. This exposure often devastates the lesser of the two halves. Let's say she's a mental moron with big boobs and a great ass. He owns a spectacular personality, a gigantic brain, nice features and a small penis. Guess who loses? The lure of the group totally negates whatever special warmth their private love making produced in the past. Pure animal sex is fine but not as a steady diet in various cages. The swinger who starts on an occasional fling will find the maintenance of his social life a bit difficult if he accidentally pounces upon a pair of blabbermouths who take pride in their adventures and spill their guts to a friend who tells other friends. Friends may ostracize them at their old haunts, even though secretly envious of what they think is the ultimate assignation (what do they know?) but fear guilt by association. Swingers lose jobs and trust and soon find that, while tennis and bowling represent togetherness, their new sport is more of a separator.

A couple, now divorced and living in Europe, provide suitable examples of how swinging can distort a relationship. This couple's bizarre actions once they entered the swinging world is certainly extreme but worth examining as I observed other couples following the same routine to a lesser degree. Their names are fictitious but the story is true.

Don suggested swinging to Louise after their third anniversary. "Just his weird sense of humor," she thought, but began believing him as he pursued his desires. Don and Louise, both good looking by any standards, shared a common restlessness and an interest in sex. In fact, their insatiable sexual appetites prompted Louise to finally agree. Neither of them knew any contacts or had any idea of what lay ahead. They first frequented a club in Los Angeles noted for its swinging clientele, who considered them the prize catch of the night. Louise began enjoying the attention men paid her while Don, the more realistic of the pair, began thinking that maybe this wasn't such a good idea. But, too late. As their visits continued, Louise became the aggressor. Now intolerably egotistical, she acted like the whole of her existence rested upon her visits to the club. They broke the ice after some weeks attending their first party.

By this time, Louise had supplemented her adequate wardrobe with clothes she felt she needed to make herself as desirable as possible, demolishing their budget. Don's jealousy flared after each party, making Louise feel even more important. "I must be the most beautiful woman in the room," she thought. Next came cosmetic surgery to correct her slightly flabby stomach. She went even further by having breast implants and her thighs trimmed. She discarded glasses for contact lenses in three colors. She became the self-elected queen of the swingers, dragging Don along like an albatross.

Don's vengeance was cruel and thoughtless. He planned a party of his own, thinking he would teach her a lesson. As the party progressed with Louise enjoying her one-on-one sex, four men and two women entered the room at Don's request, then violated Louise in the most degrading manner, causing her bodily harm. The divorce, initiated by Louise, followed soon after. She told the court about the events leading up to her divorce, causing both of them extreme embarrassment and Don, the loss of his job.

The debacle forced Louise's character flaws to the surface during this period of her life. She needed psychiatric help, something her husband could not provide in his angered and hurt frame of mind.

I can dismiss working in sex clinics as a scientific approach to problems. Avoid these places for extras, unless you feel like volunteering as a partner who helps the deprived. If you possess this social worker syndrome, it might work for you.

A new trend on the medical horizon might provide the answer for the more timid and less aggressive cheater. Love therapists, formerly known as plain old shrinks, occupy penthouses in fashionable medical buildings. For anywhere from seventy dollars for a psychologist to two hundred dollars for a psychiatrist, you can be analyzed and screwed, or cut out the analyzing altogether and really get your money's worth in a forty-five-minute session. This approach offers definite advantages unless paying for it causes a hangup.

This trend gives you a chance to shop the market, picking out the shrink who turns you on or even a pair of practitioners if you can afford it. You'll enjoy lively conversation, considering his educational background. Relax. Forget your worries about making the first move, or responding to the initial bite on the neck. It's his specialty, like gynecology or proctology for other physicians, and his instincts will lead him in the right direction. He can also show you, because of his vast experience, positions you never knew existed. Motel rooms and other private trysting places disappear. Also, your weekly appointment negates chasing each other around with secret coded telephone calls and never coinciding your meeting times because of babysitters and his busy work schedule. The romantic aspects seem a bit dim, but you definitely lessen your chances of getting caught. The doctor won't send you love letters or flowers that can trip you up. You will receive only one thing by mail—his bill that your husband pays.

I think that, for the beginner, this sort of arrangement represents a good jumping-off point. If you can handle your guilt about your husband paying for your infidelity, you can handle anything.

I personally never went this route, although some of my friends did. They stumbled upon these shrinks by accident, thinking their treatment valid. I can't see the medical value of internal therapy for claustrophobia. I did, however, see the practical side, as I outlined above. If you choose this kind of "help," first develop a whopping neurosis, manifest its symptoms expertly for your husband, keep it up for the doctor's sake and enjoy. Never tell the professional that he is a human dildo; it will violate his ethics. He needs your basic mental problem as his erection launch.

"A woman's tongue can be a useful tool in bed, but it can become her own worst enemy."

CHAPTER 3

Friends and Other Myths

A woman's tongue can be a useful tool in bed, but when she rolls it out like a New Year's Eve noisemaker, it becomes her own worst enemy. *What's that?* Did I hear a groan of discontent emanating from your lips, dear reader? Consider some of these more common fables:

A. I've just snagged the most gorgeous guy with four-hour staying power. He can come seven times in as many positions in one session. I must tell someone what I've found. *No one will believe you. At the next party you don't attend, guess who the revelers jokingly describe as your fantasy figure. You'll be nicknamed Wonderwoman and Superman. This story should make the rounds like a flash flood. If any of the ladies believe you, their envy will outweigh any loyalty unless you promise them some of the action. If you told them about some impotent schnook with a two-inch penis who works for the*

Department of Sanitation, you might enjoy some protection because of their happiness over your failure.

B. Ms. W. doesn't know my friends the way I do. How dare she condemn my chums who wouldn't hurt me for the world. Her pals must be the average gossipy cats. *Even if your friends consisted of Joan of Arc, Nancy Reagan and three nuns, I still advocate a permanent state of lockjaw in this area, based on my experience. Let's assume your friends dedicate their lives to keeping you safe from harm. They'd face a firing squad rather than see one hair on your head pulled out. They're perfect, but never forget, they're human. It's harder for them to shut up about you screwing your Maytag service guy than all the codes you learned in the Secret Service. Nobody wants you exposed, but how can it hurt anything if they keep the secret within the group? But someone in your group must be a member of another group who doesn't even know you. The news spreads like spilled detergent until it soaks the poor drip who uses it.*

Beware the deadly motherly instinct. Your good friend knows for sure that you're heading toward total destruction. You've never been happier, or looked more radiant. She sees this as a temporary state before you collapse into a mental hospital. For your own good and after months of sincere soul-searching, she decides she'll help you. So, after telling your husband about your sickness, she watches the men in white carry you away, knowing she did the right thing, only too late.

C. My best girlfriend helped me plan the strategy that hooked him. How can I rob her of the victory celebration by remaining silent? *If*

21

your girlfriend worked so hard helping you, she'll decide that at least you could have taken her along for a threesome. Don't worry much about excluding her. I can only imagine a rank beginner asking another woman for help in seducing a man she doesn't know. Her advice could easily wreck the plan. If she knows his identity and can nail you with name, time and place, I suggest you take a typhoid shot and head for the Middle East. I'd rather take my chances on the Sinai Peninsula than on a broad with all that information.

D. For years, two of my best friends told me all about their affairs. I never told on them, so why should they tell on me? Besides, I could bury them with all of the evidence. That will keep them quiet. *I can relate to this situation. Just because you're not a spiller of beans, what makes you so sure they're in your league? We sometimes project the best and worst qualities in ourselves onto the people closest to us. We pride ourselves on choosing friends wisely, then hope it doesn't make us look like prize jerks if we pick a loser.*

Before I even began my life of wanton wanting, a cherished friend was well into it. Sandra, as I'll call her, recounted her exciting trysts with great wit and charm, two of her best qualities besides a knockout body and face. The itch hadn't caught up with me yet, so I enjoyed her stories without enviously wishing she'd climax herself to death.

After two years of listening, I invented, as a joke, an elaborate, inconceivably wild affair of my own. Something to top anything she had done. I planned a serious one-hour exposé of erotic craziness ending with a ludicrous punch line.

I chose a person we both knew: madly attractive and much coveted in our circle of friends, yet unattainable. I had written, rewritten and rehearsed my enormous lie for weeks. It became so believable, I was sure I could relate it with complete authenticity and a straight face.

I began by describing his insatiable, strange desire for my body, something he had been fantasizing about for years. The torment of denial finally took precedence over reason as he propositioned me in the skating rink cafeteria while the rest of our collective families took their favorite Sunday exercise. Of course, I was not to be taken easily. He pursued me through weeks of weenie roasts, a funeral that we all attended, and a ride on a merry-go-round with the calliope drowning out his begging from the innocent ears of our kiddies. We consummated the affair at a beach house he rented for the afternoon, costing him four hundred dollars, because he knew of my passion for the pounding surf. The description of the actual seduction made the love affair between Romeo and Juliet look like a casual encounter. His kisses began with each toenail, traveling around the body and eventually missing not an inch of my scalp. He would have gone for each hair follicle had time not been a factor.

I thought by this time Sandra had my number and "You're putting me on" was only seconds away. I evidently overestimated her intelligence, or possibly intelligence remains buried where a female's ego is concerned. Whatever the reason, I confessed, but I could not convince her than my story was a fabrication. The bedeviled beauty who had seduced every man she went after except this one had a

23

colossal bug up her ass. Her anger was immediate and her vengeance swift. She bombarded her husband at dinner, saying I was the bottom-feeder in the neighborhood, and had been for years. "That butter-wouldn't-melt-in-her-mouth lady deserves shunning by the entire neighborhood," she told him. Not only was I a prize libertine, I had also suggested that she follow me into the wicked world I loved. Sandra's craziness seemed tame compared with her husband's fury, judging from an unpleasant call my husband received that evening. Mr. Sandra informed him that I was not allowed within ten miles of his pure, offended wife. Her casting of the first stone vitiated whatever accusations I might have directed at her to kill her credibility. The fuming husband withheld her imaginary list of my lovers and her description of the sordid filth while ranting at my husband. (Remember the male fraternity I spoke of earlier? Incriminating a mutual friend simply wasn't cricket.) Had my husband believed all of this, I could not have used it in this text. He knew full well that I was not a common trollop, so an explanation from me proved quite unnecessary.

Had Sandra used her head and accused me of only one indiscretion, my fate might have been sealed. One affair he might believe—hundreds are ridiculous. Her expulsion from our circle of friends was immediate. She's gone but not forgotten, like the bubonic plague.

E. A lot of the fun of living dangerously is sharing your wickedness with other people. I feel so much more attractive when half the world knows how I'm pursued. *Both sexes employ this kind of ego building frequently. The instinct for approval of beauty and youth drives many people into extramarital affairs. It's the worst reason, but understandable. Both men and women want the opposite sex to find them attractive. Many great film beauties, whom kings and tycoons pursue across continents, become objects of envy. Analyze the state of their lives, however, and you may forgo trading your tract house for their problems. Consider the negative aspects of their lives. If you want half the world to know about your fling, your husband probably will be in that half. Check out other ways of achieving stardom if you need the buildup. Take a doctorate in astronomy with seventy male classmates panting at your heels. This is a safe way of extracting envy from your peers. If you need the ultimate adoration, convince your husband that the budget isn't stretching and take a job as a stripper. Take any lengths of soothing your battered ego short of cheating by advertising with billboards.*

People will judge you severely for your perceived wicked lifestyle even if your romance qualifies as the tenderest, most beautiful experience. Only you and your lover know what occurs in bed, and others will only half hear any explanation you may offer and distort it as it spreads by the grapevine. It's not fun.

"He calmy asked, 'What kind of affair do you want?'"

CHAPTER 4

This Is My First Affair, So Please Be Kind

This book mainly targets beginners and intermediates. Successfully unfaithful women might find a few brush-up tips but not much that they didn't discover for themselves the hard way. Ladies who feel like they're stepping on eggshells, however, need primers with practical examples. My first affair in retrospect was both disastrous and hilarious.

First, some background. Statistics show that infidelity is on the rise among women in the thirty-to-sixty-year age group. The upswing is being pushed by libbies so sophisticated they probably wouldn't get caught robbing Tiffany's at high noon. Career women are able to get away with a lot more hanky panky. They traipse around day and night with corporate meetings at odd hours. Their business sense makes them craftier and better organized. They also can screen a variety of men who cross their paths at work. This puts them one step ahead of the housewife. Both types of women share two challenging factors: the times in which they live and the time in which they were born.

The forty-to-sixty-year-olds grew up before the sexual revolution, when virginity was not a dirty word and a silver wedding anniversary seemed a common blessing rather than a prehistoric curse. Some of us more flexible souls can intellectually comprehend reversal of roles, marital infidelity, and decadent offspring. We even recognize kindred females as sexually liberated sharks sniffing around the bodies of bleeding men left that way by the barracudas. Yes, we envision this,

27

but few of us can participate successfully. Caught in mid-generation, stuck with outmoded morals, we confront constant temptation by the highly publicized delights of the devil and the deep, deep throat.

Until my thirty-second year, I remained faithful to my husband in mind and body. As I approached thirty-four, my faithfulness began dissipating. An outgoing personality and zest for living convinced our friends that my action exceeded the hottest crap table in Las Vegas. I would have sworn in blood at the outset of our marriage, consumed by overwhelming "love," that I would not be a negative Kinsey statistic.

My life focused on the human relationship. I like people of both sexes and associate myself equally with men and women. My husband had many women friends, so the jealousy factor never caused a severe problem although, as in all marriages, it cropped up from time to time with the appropriate screaming and accusations. We were sexually compatible, having interests in common and apart: the raising of two children, with very different viewpoints on how to accomplish this task; and mortgage miseries. For two years I lived with agonizing confusion. The books I read and movies I saw told me, okay, act like that "slut," the one my mother wouldn't let me chat with in my old neighborhood. In school, one wild chick always kept us bug-eyed. Suddenly the wild chick was chic, and good girls finished last.

Achieving my fantasy only required reading available manuals, dumping my guilts, finding a suitable man and not getting caught. "You must become skillfully predatory without losing your femininity," I told myself. "Keep you husband satisfied even after a terrific matinee with Mr. X, and cope with the screaming demands of the kids as you arrive in the driveway with your lover's semen dripping down your left thigh." With aid from someone like Germaine Greer during my apprenticeship, I might have sidestepped the indignities I encountered on the yellow brick road to promiscuity.

Dick Haymes kept me swooning ever since he caught Betty Grable in mid-song falling off a library ladder in an over-budgeted 1940s musical. Dick, though, represented an unattainable fantasy. I'd filed and indexed Chuck Crane in the same category before I began growing my fangs.

Chuck sparkled as emcee, singer, and witty ad-libber in a local saloon. The owner always introduced him as "Charming Chuck, the Motel Athlete." He ignored his quivering superfan sitting cross-legged, chin in hands, dabbing at the Pavlovian saliva triggered by his baritone.

After careful deliberation, I selected Charming Chuck as my first hit-the-sack adventure. But I needed an accomplice. Doing this solo seemed unthinkable at this stage. I chose Cynthia, a classy lady of low moral fiber who would take this opportunity to search and seize, making her a safe bet to keep her mouth shut.

By the time both of our husbands simultaneously left town on business, my act practically shone from its polish. We entered the Radar Room, electing to sit at the oval bar near the entertainers' tables. I made the first move, complimenting Chuck on his performance. Chuck reciprocated by offering the "pretty lady" a drink. After an hour of chatting, sipping and occasional applause by Cynthia and me for an act neither of us listened to, Chuck had spilled his life story. The highlights included a touching tale of recent divorce, support of five children, two jobs other than his club act, just managing to keep body and soul together, a sinus problem, and impending hernia surgery. I gave my first name, a glowing definitive statement on my blissful marriage, two Tylenol for his sinus headache relief, good advice on health insurance, and copious sympathy about his present predicaments.

It's amazing, I thought, watching this idol of sexuality shove a Dristan atomizer up his left nostril seeking relief before his big number, how images shatter. Just a fleeting blemish, I decided, remembering that stars are also human beings.

The evening progressed with Chuck creeping at a snail's pace toward a proposition. I played the role of the nice lady rather than the type one might consider a quickie chickie. Considering that time was not on my side because of my husband making infrequent trips, I decided to punt and hope for the best. Initially, I hadn't figured on making the proposition; receiving one would have been so much easier to handle.

My friend at this point began sharing a chair with an overweight tenor and making it look very easy.

There was no controlling the tone of my outburst, although I made a valiant attempt at portraying a sophisticated Tiger Lady as I carefully enunciated, "I think we should have an affair," hoping it needed no echo. As it turned out, though, his reply of "I beg your pardon?" necessitated another go-round.

I achieved some control but wondered whether to lighten or intensify. Too much mind control might ruin my acting and reacting ability, so I relied on instinct, charging to the five-yard line, setting up a score.

Luck was with me; Chuck did not run for the safety of the men's room. Instead, he calmly asked, "Do you know what kind of affair you want?" I never knew a choice existed. Deferring to his obvious knowledge on the subject, I asked, "Describe a few, including your favorite kind, so we might arrive at something mutually gratifying."

His large black eyes stared at mine interminably as he rocked his body to the music, clapping his hands and stomping his feet. He finally smiled, running his hands over my shoulders in a friendly way. Touchdown, with the extra point.

From that moment, it became evident as we chatted that here sat a Lothario with the bold and easy-going traits for which I longed.

"Why me?" he asked. "There must be more exciting men you could pick for your first time out."

It was my turn to stare. "There are?"

He answered that nonchalant throw-away line in true Double 07 style. "There aren't."

Chuck escorted me to my car and properly, if decorously, molested me in the front seat. He gave me his phone number at both jobs. "I work from 10 a.m. to 2 a.m., but I can see you for lunch."

What a setup! No problems with robbing my hubby of his evenings when I could entertain at lunch.

Two weeks dragged by with the difficulty factor increasing each day. Why did I have to do everything? When I finally dialed the number, his bouncy hello made my misgivings almost evaporate. It bothered me, though, when he asked, "Who is this?"

My identification echoed rather foolishly. "This is…the girl you sat with at the Radar Room and walked to the car, and…"

"And I remember you. How'd you get my number?"

"You gave it to me," I feebly replied, feeling pangs of guilt as if he were the married one who didn't want to be tracked.

We spoke for a short while, then I mentioned lunch. He made valid excuses for his limited time, "But will you please keep trying until I have a free hour?" he added. Two more calls that week received the same rejection followed by, "Don't give up."

Frustrated at failing the Cosmo test thus far, I opted for a blitzing momentum and made one more call.

I don't want to have lunch with you, Chuck."

"I'm sorry to hear that, dear."

"I want to go to bed with you, Chuck."

"You happened to catch me on a good day. I'm free at 1:30. Find a nice room near my office, call and give me the details. We'll enjoy each other."

That gave me exactly two hours for hair, clothes and accommodations arrangements. A careful inspection of my closet revealed what the well-dressed wife and mommy wears. With no time for Frederick's, I chose slacks and a turtleneck.

Cleopatra's handmaidens anointed her with rare scented oils. I settled for my husband's Aramis due to an allergy to scented vapors, with no sweet-smelling $50-an-ounce in sight.

A small suspicion surfaced: This isn't the way my dreams took place. But I rationalized it out of existence by a firm belief that an affair with Chuck promised me equality, responsibility, and a compliment on my coping ability.

I called the auto club, checking on suitable motels in his area. I settled on the one with the king-size bed. The manager assured me that his was the finest, cleanest and most beautiful motel "for my relatives who are flying in from New York."

Talk about smarts. I parked my car across the alley from the Sunset Pines Motel, obtained the key and raced across the street, calling Chuck from the Bouncing Ball Bar. Clever girls do not use the room phone—no evidence. He estimated an arrival in thirty minutes, giving me enough time to unwind and prepare.

Thank goodness a railing encircled the balcony, offering a degree of safety, or I might have been a headline in the evening edition. The room seemed squeezed by dismal, fraying, faded green walls and the nondescript furniture. These downers plus the absence of blackout curtains precipitated a major anxiety attack while I hung backwards over the balcony's protective steel slats, the key rattling against the bars like the tin cups prisoners use to protest their environment. I could only hope our passion would change the frog room into a handsome prince.

The knock interrupted my nap. The door opened and Chuck walked past me, tossing his jacket on the chair while making a brief survey.

"Nice," he said. "Very nice," and he meant it. With just four steps, Chuck made it from the door to the john, which boasted great acoustics.

He emerged, fly open, with one leg out of his trousers, revealing the latest in St. Tropez net briefs.

"Sorry I'm late; business is crazy," said the naked man to the well-dressed stiff lady on the verge of psychiatric catatonia.

The Motel Athlete's new record for disrobing only increased his partner's advancing case of *rigor mortis*. My attempt at sophisticated stripping produced one sweater caught in an earring until both came free in spastic unison. My slacks' departure from the lower portion of my body revealed the forgotten, oh-so-glamourous knee-high socks I'd substituted for torn pantyhose, then in an attitude of wild abandon the neat creature of habit hung her clothes carefully in the closet.

Once in bed, however, the role players knew their parts, tangoing expertly together like Arthur and Katherine Murray capturing the hearts of middle America. During the foreplay we stroked the other's appropriate parts with Chuck blossoming in full flower. Thank goodness nature spares the female of the species from proving her passion, I thought. My unnatural state didn't result from guilt or fear, and it certainly wasn't a poor performance on Chuck's part. He glided magnificently from one major sex act to another like a classic Baryshnikov *pas de deux*. I felt a kind of detachment.

"What can I do to make you happy?" he asked.

My answer stopped him somewhere between the navel and earlobe.

"Check us into the Beverly Hills Hotel, order some wine, spend an hour trying to seduce me draped over a Chinese silk lounge, and stop biting my big toe. I hate that."

He spent the next twenty minutes repairing his wounded ego with repeated explanations of his financial problems and a close inspection of his fresh hernia scar. I assured him it wasn't his deformed body, as he put it, that turned me off.

I slipped under the sheets as Chuck, dressing quickly, assured me our next encounter would be easier. "We'll know each other better," he said. My cynical retort pertaining to his forty-five-minute hot box lunch made not even a dent in his ramblings about our future together.

Mr. Charming's exit line, "Be a good girl now," seemed mundane, to say the least.

"I've just been a bad girl," I said.

"No, sweetie, you were really very good."

I spent an hour relieving my pent-up anger by finishing the peeling job on the walls until the room became as grotesque as I felt.

On my way through the lobby, the desk clerk informed me he'd forgotten to ask for the money in advance and would I please pay it now? That much equality I didn't need.

My affair dangerously coincided with my ovulating cycle, now on the downgrade. If I pursued future misadventures, the Pill would have to become a part of my life. My husband's vasectomy necessitated some highly imaginative lying to the doctor about my present menopausal state, complete with hot flashes and the need for the Pill to elevate the hormone level.

The doctor's enigmatic smile reduced me to something less than Linda Lovelace (remember her?). I spent the next month on the Pill munching saltines for the morning sickness that lasted all day. Coping with breakthrough bleeding scared the hell out of me. The worst part came with sleep—a nightmare consisting of my husband bludgeoning me with a twelve-foot blue pill case. The only alternative to the Pill was a personal questionnaire mailed to every male in Southern California, with a stamped return envelope, inquiring about the vasectomy they had, plus a request for dates, names of doctors and permission to check the validity of their statements. Considering the paperwork involved, the Pill, even with the possibility of sudden death due to a blood clot, seemed the only way to go.

As I continued my search for sexual freedom, I found it was the male prerogative when the time came for asking *the* question. Those without the cut would inquire about the precautions *I* take. Some switch, I thought, from the terrorized boys in my past dying a thousand deaths at the drugstore counter waiting for the three-pack of Trojans.

The dumbest segment of this farce I save for last. I told Chuck at the outset and with deep sincerity that he ranked as the first man to gather my lilies since I took my marriage vows. I later discovered that this kind of naïve confession, besides being none of a paramour's business, also reaffirms his absolute belief you have racked up more mileage than Apollo Twelve.

If I were the heroine of a Hollywood flick, moviegoers would describe me as an unsympathetic character. My infidelity was not based on an alcoholic, wife-beating brute. I simply wanted more, a reason men have used since I grew ears. Whatever your reasons, you can profit from the gross errors I made, reducing the danger to its lowest level.

Before I discuss the technical errors, let's consider the bungling, disjointed picture I displayed. I often wonder as I look back: Could I have saved myself considerable embarrassment by going for a man I worshipped? Had I honed my skills, the possibility exists that I could have steered the afternoon's events into something less horrendous. From the outset in the nightclub, I presented myself and my wishes in a fashion that proved wrong for me.

My recollection of the incident is vivid. The almost exact dialogue shows how two perfect strangers can remain that way even after intercourse. I showed no sign of any warmth or femininity although I possess both of these qualities by the ton. I just focused too much on hurrying us into bed. I blurted out the proposition coldly, in a businesslike manner, because of fearing rejection. I wanted to say it quickly, shut my eyes and run like hell if he answered, "No."

Men have wrestled with rejection for years because society has dictated that they must make the first move. I can recall turning down many a date because I felt like I was being bought. I can now sympathize with and appreciate men's fears since I joined the game. One must learn from mistakes and turn them into victories.

It is possible to make a sexual contact in ten minutes without actually discussing the details and go to bed successfully the same day if you both present yourselves honestly, easily and without hang-ups. You can't control his initial attitude, but your attitude, if it is honest, can change and help his. When you show yourself without false trappings and he doesn't react in a pleasing manner, save yourself the bother of experimenting with failure as I did.

If the chemistry clicks, you can pretty well tell he knows what you want and wants the same thing. It doesn't always work, but it's better than role playing.

Wait a minute, some of you may be thinking: This whole business is a lot of bother and responsibility. Let him take the initiative. Let him have the problem of solving the mystery that is you.

Some people believe that never saying what you mean or being who you are rate as great fun in the beginning of a relationship. This medieval attitude causes marital discontent between two people who get together only to discover two strangers, thereby creating the need to cheat because the marriage stinks. What's the point of perpetuating the multi-personality myth?

I would have avoided the spastic disrobing and emotional alienation with Chuck had I felt comfortable when making the contract. My actions resembled those of the popular gooney bird who moves in concentric circles until it flies up its own asshole and disappears.

My business errors included:

A. Never take another female along if there exists even the slightest hint of carrying on. If you can't go it alone, you're not ready.

B. People seeing you with a possible lover in a public place is bad enough. When they see you with a man you openly panted around in the presence of your husband—even if the man seems the world's most unattainable item—the situation becomes potentially explosive.

C. Avoid taking a chance on an unknown quantity. Although I admired Chuck on stage, I knew nothing of his character. He could have been a Hannibal Lecter. Assessing the qualities of a lover you have never been with may appear daunting, but you'll sharply decrease your chances of getting into something rank if you gather some knowledge of him, however small.

D. Being seen at the check-in desk probably rates as my worst *faux pas*. Let the man make the arrangements and wait for you. It's safer, and, in my case, I could have saved half my weekly allowance.

E. I chose a motel near his work; it also bordered my husband's place of business. In my frenzied passion, the thought of my husband seeing me enter or exit had slipped my mind. It's tough enough giving the rest of the world the slip, especially if you're a popular gal, without adding your spouse's high-recognition element to the list.

The Angel of Infidelity obviously guided my steps that day. My hypochondriac bedmate expected another tryst. He classified me as a live one on the hook with no intention of letting go. How could he know after the stupidity I exhibited that he was dealing with a high-IQ novice? I lacked know-how on motel frolics, but I'm a quick study on people.

Trying not to alienate me, he never called my home. What I received instead were calls from his friends with fourth-grade-level questions: "Are you alone?" "When can he see you again? Same time, same place?"

The obvious reaction—panic—would have led me into an inescapable trap. The calls left me nervous but poised. I ran a risk in seeing him again, and it seemed greater risk if I didn't. We met again on his ground at the Radar Room. In a low B-movie scene with enough corn to choke all the Pilgrims at Plymouth Rock, I came on like Shirley Temple meeting Tarzan.

With even the lousiest performance, any lady can dump a man if she leans hard enough, endangering his freedom. I sailed in on the good ship *Lollipop*, fawning over Chuck, the man in my life who would take care of me in sickness and in health. Needless to say, Chuckie disappeared into the trees with his loincloth flapping. I came out of this experience unscathed because of luck and his inability to think past his ding dong. Don't rely too heavily on luck. The house usually wins.

You'll discover the first affair is always the toughest. Fear of the unknown often brings out the bungler in us. "Aha," you say, "I can improvise and perform without stage fright." You, my friend, devoid of fear and clutching the world by the balls, will always get caught first. A little niggling terror and self-doubt keeps you on your toes and thinking.

Sometimes it's like two parts of a jigsaw puzzle fitting perfectly into place. All the expert magazines declare the rockets' red glare and bombs bursting in air occur as soon as you hit the sheets, as long as you follow their advice on makeup and nail care. It seems more logical, however, that two strange bodies meeting for the first time in the horizontal position require some exploring and practice before the bombs become spectacular.

If you forge ahead with the bursting-bomb vision, disappointment will erase any future you may have enjoyed together. Don't expect perfection. A little skepticism, coupled with a touch of optimism, can steady you through the first round. With this kind of ambivalence, you'll live through the worst that you sort of expected anyway, or reach round two because you half expected it to be as nice as it was. Acquiring this attitude isn't easy, but consider it almost mandatory for protecting your fragile ego.

"The doctor I chose hated the pill."

CHAPTER 5
The Pill

In the previous chapter I discussed my decision to go on the Pill. For those of you already practicing birth control, skip this chapter. Some of us, however, must contend with a past blessing and present problem.

The vasectomy rate is skyrocketing. The reason? So many babies come along by accident. Our second child was conceived despite the use of a diaphragm. Afterward, my husband couldn't wait for his hysterectomy. All of his friends, being well put together mentally, had visited the guillotine without fear of losing their manhood. The Pill at this time was not widely used. Our protection included foam, diaphragms, thermometers, calendars, guessing at ovulating pains, and madonnas for prayerful supplication. If your husband eschewed the vasectomy and a present lover shared your fallopian tubes with your mate, a baby didn't represent a major catastrophe—except for its birth.

Even after consistent use of these precautions, surprise pregnancies raised some eyebrows, but you blamed it on your husband's exceptional sperm strength. The little devils sneaked by all that armor. He became a hero in his misery with another mouth to feed. With the advent of the Pill and still no vasectomy, the upper hand was definitely yours.

The Pill began the sexual revolution. Common sense told me that. I didn't need an expert. All the he's could make babies, and the fortunate she's who weren't prone to blood clots could refuse the offer.

Concerned husbands and fretful wives who did not like the Pill because of side effects elected vasectomies. It's amazing how many women who previously declined the Pill now suddenly gobble one a day. How does one explain this new-found love for the Pill to a husband who risked life and limb in a simple thirty-minute surgery? If you can still make babies and choose to pursue outside sex without it, I consider you too inane to grasp anything in this book.

The affair with Chuck seemed incredulous considering my savvy. I went through the entire routine without giving it a thought. So you might say I fall into the ex-inane group, although I vindicated myself by simply visiting my doctor, but complications followed that visit.

The Pill is a habit one must acquire. No matter how bright your head, it's not something you think about before you hit the sack, so swallow one at precisely the same time each day so that if you miss even once the panic that strikes will cause a simulated coronary.

My next encounter was a flashing moment of passion three days before my gynecological appointment. The affair was proceeding on a calm and lovely sea of glazed passion definitely leading toward a crashing breaker until I remembered. My memory cells activated and preceded the penetration by about two minutes. I really liked him but not enough to carry his child.

As I leaned up on one elbow, cradling my left cheek with a shaky hand, the explanation began. You can't pull this off, though, with grace and sophistication unless you forgo the explanation and refuse intercourse because of your burning desire for fellatio.

As I began speaking seriously, I saw his boat slowly pulling away from the harbor. "We can't screw," I said. Not wishing to destroy a relationship that could develop into something superior, I indulged in the numbers game with a virtual stranger. This is not something I normally do. I enjoy exotic lovemaking the most with men I like a great deal. As it turned out, he became one of those men. There had been three, counting my husband.

He couldn't believe his good fortune. I discovered from him and a later survey of my more talky friends that fellatio is employed but not enjoyed by many women. Once you start it, the relationship turns sour if you quit. So hang from the baboons' family tree with your dumb explanation, rather than begin something you find distasteful. If he's a nice guy, he'll only reduce you to the high school level by asking for a hand job. If he's one in a million, he'll put your feelings before his penis and go away quietly. Jot his number in your mental notebook and call when it's safe.

When is it safe? One hundred percent safe can never apply to you. I am speaking now of contraceptive measures. The Pill fails in two percent of all users. If you're enough of a gambler to indulge in extramarital sex, ninety-eight percent odds should qualify as safe enough. I abstained during the mid-portion of my cycle for extra safety.

Other methods of birth control may suit the compulsive gamblers or ladies who cheat with the subconscious urge of getting caught.

You'll read more about these misguided creatures later in the book. If you're a new user, do not step out until after popping the Pill for at least one cycle. Two would be better.

Introducing the alien pill case into the home might prove sticky. If you have been using other methods, your husband will probably welcome the newcomer even with its side effects. If you are in the vasectomy group, consider taking a ten-week course at the Actors Studio before explanation time is due. If you try hiding it in other kinds of medicine bottles or slinking into the bathroom like one of the ten most wanted fugitives, you run a real risk. Even if it's the first box and you're not yet guilty, your husband's discovery of the Pill without prior knowledge will convict you as surely as if he discovered a videotape of a Roman orgy with you as the star. If you can't convincingly place it in the medicine chest along with the aspirin and make a respectable pill out of a whorish tablet, my advice: give it up or pay the price.

Start your new life by living your first lie well. It's the least dangerous lie. If it doesn't go well and you're forced to flush the remaining pills down the john, all you endure is nagging suspicion for a few weeks.

You'll live many lies in your chosen lifestyle, and each one must be accompanied by quick thinking, ingenuity and, in grave emergencies, a poker face.

The best approach? Make your family doctor insist that you go on the Pill immediately. The responsibility is no longer yours. Deceiving a busy practitioner is not terribly difficult. Try a specialist who doesn't know you. Your husband will agree that you deserve the finest opinion.

If your husband is a doctor, mail this book back to the publisher for a full refund.

Doctors write prescriptions like you write checks. Describe your pre-menopausal symptoms after applying makeup that gives you a Camille-like pallor. Scream about your hemorrhaging that never happens during an office visit. I don't think your medical man will insist on spending three weeks of his vacation in your bathroom waiting for the big event. Become cranky and slightly wacky before your period, extending the symptoms. Scream for regulation in your life. You can't go on suffering and inconveniencing the family. This approach, plus the implied threat of terminal PMS, will usually get the job done.

My husband presented no problem, but the doctor I chose hated the Pill. He lost one patient in ten thousand with a clot and got sued. He tried persuading me I'd be better off crazy than dead, and stubbornly insisted that withholding the medication was for my own good. He made me sign a form releasing him from all responsibility in the event his prescription caused my demise. All medication carries some risk, and as luck would have it I chose the anal-retentive with forty forms for everything from penicillin to Ex-Lax. This is highly unusual, but you may as well be prepared for any complication.

By the time I glommed onto that dispenser with my hot little hands, I could hardly wait for the end of my cycle and the debut of my debauchery. Into my second week, however, with the all-day morning sickness that sometimes accompanies the benefits, I thought of quitting. The doctor seemed happy when I reported my miseries, and as a result of that sanguine reaction, I continued popping the Pill—out of spite. By the third week, the nausea subsided and I once again remembered why I sought them in the first place.

An acquaintance of mine concocted another story that worked. She maneuvered her husband into persuading her that she needed the Pill. During a three-month interval she adroitly worked her family into a panic by gruesomely recalling two pregnancies caused by cut husbands. The wives, as she described them, qualified as Mother Superior types. Preying on her husband's distrust of doctors in general—especially the one that snipped him—she secured the Pill prescription. After she fought tooth and nail, her husband finally shoved Pill One down her throat.

You know your man. Choose the scenario that he can accommodate best. Some husbands wouldn't know if you were taking quinine for an advanced case of malaria. If he's your man, you'll enjoy easy going, even reading this book in bed while he's biting his toenails.

"My stomach became a sack of baseballs."

CHAPTER 6
The Reflection

Mirror, mirror on the wall. Who is the fairest of them all? If you're a good lady and have decent self-esteem, the answer should be— YOU. I know it's you, you know it's you, but we are dealing with millennium reality. If you desire a bit of fooling around in this decade, the answer is Brooke Shields, the Statue of Liberty replacement for our symbol of freedom and opportunity. "Give me your tired, your poor. The huddled masses yearning to be free." Bullshit. Give me a perfect set of tits and ass in tight Calvins and I'll show you freedom.

Am I angry about this absolute fact? You bet I am, and I have lots of company. Fighting back by staying fat and frumpy will frustrate all of us, however. We'll balloon and eat our peanut butter and jelly alone instead of champagne and caviar in a fine restaurant with a cheatee. (He is, after all, a cheatee, if we are the cheater.)

You must accept this universal word without cringing if you long for success. A good friend says, "I am surviving, not cheating." Surviving is a by-product of cheating for her, as it is for many women. She endures a marriage with a boring, babbling drunk. Financial problems prevent her from leaving, and I suspect she wouldn't leave even if she solved her national debt. She pirouettes around her problems, never facing with truth or realism what she's become, what she does, or what lies in the future. This kind of Last

Tango in the San Fernando Valley produces confusion, and confusion results in getting caught.

Put this book down now and go to your mirror for a good hard look, and come back. Chances are, if you are honest with yourself, you need a hundred-thousand-mile tune-up. You take care of your car. Think of yourself as a vehicle that will take you where you want to go without leaking oil or stalling on a steep grade. Always think up— positive. Some of us are Rolls Royces, some Toyotas. But, damn it, even if you are a go-cart, be the best go-cart you can be.

You're in training now. Basic training in the army takes six weeks of discipline and rigorous exercise. Discipline is the key word here. If you lack discipline in your personal life, how can you employ it in your cheating life? Every professional criminal plans her caper carefully—taking into consideration every detail of what she hopes is her perfect crime. She analyzes, plans, perfects and ultimately commits. Society brands us as criminals if we cheat, so start thinking like the Mafia. You may not wind up with a laundry or numbers racket, but I guarantee you won't get busted for pornography, even if you star in your own personal movie.

All right, you are now thinking like a Godmother. Godfathers can look like overstuffed, long dead, unembalmed mooses and have nineteen-year-old, beautiful long-legged Bambis curled up in their forest every night. You can't. You can't fight the system, and the system says you must look good. After giving this fact of life much thought, I still can't come up with a reason. You can buy a beautiful boy body even if you look like shit, but who wants to buy? It's tough

51

enough buying a salami sandwich with the escalating cost of living without shelling out for a male salami who probably won't give you value for value. Look around and see how many homely men go out with lovely women. I believe most women, either through training or genetic makeup, can see beyond the outer garb. I'm not talking about yesterday's freeway, accident, although some of us loftier thinkers picture Quasimodo as a beautiful being based on the goodness of his soul. I am referring to nice men who possess a good sense of humor, kindness of spirit and a generously affectionate manner who also happen to be paunchy, balding and bowlegged. We give them a chance in our lives and often love them physically as well as emotionally.

Now, think about how men talk. "What a pair of knockers," "tight ass," "tight pussy." "She has legs that go up to her neck." It's not their fault. The media programs them: masses of magazines with old Brookey on the covers; Playboy, Penthouse, ad infinitum. We have one, Playgirl, a token publication. We also have male strippers, but who among us ever takes one home? There are exceptions to every rule. I know a lady boozer with red, baggy eyes, reminiscent of a Bassett hound, who has her pick of almost any man. She possess an innate ability of exuding sexiness stemming from her massive ego and that intangible quality of hers that makes even me look past her veiny nose right into her soul. She'll be sexy at her funeral. She is an enigma.

I am not saying you must look like Ms. Shields, but you do compete with many beautiful women—many of them young or in the work world—so think accordingly. I knew a young man intimately who told me, "There's nothing as beautiful as an older woman who is well turned out. She has the dignity and grace of her years, and the looks to match." This book is certainly aimed at the thirty-five to eighty-five-year-old lady, and the media is now agreeing with this young man. The baby boom of the forties and fifties produced the woman of today who is in the majority. We finally have the numbers on our side. Linda Evans, Joan Collins and Ali McGraw are becoming the over-fifty sex symbols. They look good. They work at it. If you're thinking of cheating as an avocation, you'll do your homework. These wonderful broads are paving the way for us. This is our time and opportunity to knock the nineteen-year-olds on their perfect asses and take over the world. They can't compete with our experience in or out of bed. They may know the "now" lingo but we understand the male animal, so with a little bit of linguistic practice, some lifting and reshaping of our erogenous zones—namely T and A—and a definitive plan of action, the competition shrinks markedly.

Do not accomplish all this personal improvement overnight. If you've been wearing bowling footwear and a muumuu for twenty years, you must subtly introduce sling-back "come fuck me" shoes and Oscar de la Renta originals. You are actually doing your husband a favor. It's sort of a three-way gift. You feel better looking good. The man of the house sees you looking good most of the time, which, by the way, produces a myriad of wonderful side effects. The boyfriend, be it singular or plural, depending on your stamina, gets turned on, thereby even producing possibly more wonderful side effects. You can rationalize any illegitimate scheme into a virtuous action. Al Capone did it successfully for years until his demise due to syphilis, a social disease we will discuss in a later chapter.

If you plan on doing all of your cheating in a sleazy truck stop, your makeover won't require anything too drastic, but I feel that, if you are to grow as a person and experience the world as it is today, you should treat yourself to a variety of places and people. Don't limit yourself. Remember the Boy Scout motto, "Be prepared." I picked that up taking my kids to Scout meetings, and if memory serves, I also picked up a Scoutmaster or two. Keep your eyes and ears open. Opportunities to learn and seize are everywhere.

One of my first outings with an engineer, a rather slim and fit fellow, took place in my pre-dieting stage. I was twenty pounds overweight with most of it centered in my tummy, that spot where all excess poundage winds up. I didn't have a bad figure, but my second husband of many years no longer tried coaxing me into a bikini. We were used to each other and comfortable in our nakedness.

Getting into a state of undress with a new man after being with only one for so long is really quite uncomfortable, even with a great body. You start realizing how programmed you are when you change the channel. Suddenly you're in a bedroom with someone who takes his pants off before his shirt, unlike your husband, and it throws the scene off kilter. He's conversing and actually staring at your person while you disrobe. Your husband usually fiddles with the TV or brushes his teeth. He's seen you do this a thousand times. With your mate it's just going to bed, even if the sex is great. It's no big production. With the engineer or postman, you visit that bedroom for sex, and if it's the first time for him, it's a production in vivid color with a major hard-on before you hit the sheets. You wanted all this attention; otherwise you wouldn't be there. You're the star at last.

I assumed, being a product of the moving-picture generation, it would all fall into place. The only thing that fell was my heart—right into my already oversized stomach. I couldn't talk about the PTA or my Aunt Tillie, and the silence seemed deafening. I didn't remember how to talk dirty or romantic with a stranger. I forgot how to walk, talk, lie down, stand up, and smoke. If you're lucky, the man will know how to dance you through this rocky mating ritual. Even if he's experienced at this sort of thing, you will still stumble through it. As in any sport, time and practice will be the only cure for the bumbles. It's the rare woman who can hit a home run for the new team she's been traded to after playing shortstop for the Dodgers for fifteen years.

I suddenly became aware of all my features. Even my good parts didn't look good enough, and my stomach, a thing I hadn't really considered much for eons, became a sack of baseballs. Or so I felt. The music playing in the background seemed quite a departure from "Heeere's Johnny!" Candles illumined strategic places. He actually handed me a glass of champagne, and I sat on the floor near the bed and asked him, "Do you mind if I throw up?" It was my first day in kindergarten, and I wanted my mommy. My mommy would have thrown up, then thrashed me if she discovered what I was doing, but I didn't care. When you think death awaits, you pray; when you're scared, you want your mommy at any cost.

God, I must have looked awful, judging from his expression. He brought me a cold cloth and spoke to me quietly, when I started praying. What a jewel he was. We talked for hours about my life and what I wanted, and about his fears, which were as real as mine. After all, men are human too. My engineer had been somebody's husband at one time, and I wondered if he showed her a comparable kindness and understanding.

He lulled me into a state of peace, the ultimate result we both wanted, and the lovemaking began. The thoughts that caromed through my mind during foreplay seem ludicrous as I look back on that moment. My stomach became the focal point of my entire existence. If I kissed him on my side, my stomach looked awful because it kind of hung the wrong way, sliding toward my hip. If I lay on top of him, my stomach squished out. If I stood up, it bulged. If I knelt, it hung on the floor. I chose a supine position and held it in. If I snuff out the candles, I thought, he won't see my stretch marks.

I never moved during the entire procedure. I lay on my back looking like an upended, rigor-mortised turtle. He made all the moves. I would not budge from the safe stomach turf I had created. Some hot lover I turned out to be. I even dressed on my back.

I knew what was happening, well aware of my crazy behavior. I just couldn't segue into the next scene. What a disaster. I never saw him again, no surprise to me. If only I had met him later after three months of starving and ten million sit-ups. I was not prepared; it was like taking a final exam without studying. No confidence.

The beginning of any venture is tough enough without adding extra burdens. My stomach became such a big concern that I lugged it over into my own ballpark. My husband couldn't pry me off my back for weeks, with no explanation forthcoming. What could I tell him? My growing awareness of my body proved a good thing because I began an improvement plan of action. It resulted not from a case of massive ego but from a lady's resolve for better looks, and that's a positive step.

At first I chased the elusive "10" body with a vengeance, boring myself to death with lettuce, getting the hungry dizzies and feeling generally rotten. I calmed down as the weeks went by and found tasty recipes that didn't take eight hours of chopping and grating. I invested in a steamer that takes everything from a Martha Stewart model garden and makes it taste great. I cut out red meat, thereby reducing my grocery bill as well as my avoirdupois, and put the whole family on my diet. Again, the husband benefits. I was instrumental in preventing his potential heart attack from the crap I had been feeding him. I added weight to his wallet instead of his body, and the kids and I were looking better. This is not one of those cockeyed rationalizations I talked about earlier. This was a bona fide grade-A health effort.

I thought then, why didn't I do this without the cheating motivation? I honestly don't know the reason. Does the end justify the means? Again we come back to the criminal mind. Robin Hood stole from the rich and gave to the poor. I wasn't hurting anyone and seemed to be helping everyone. Next case.

What do you ladies prefer? Advertisers spend billions of dollars advertising self panaceas. I didn't have Richard Simmons bouncing and screaming at me on the tube. When I started this life he was a fat, unknown kid. Jane Fonda was a radical anti-war preacher instead of a work-out factory with video tapes you can play at home, and the present health craze hadn't been invented. All I had was my obese doctor, coughing his brains out from his three-pack-a-day habit, telling me to lose weight and get healthy. Tennis was something rich people played for fun; who knew it was good for you? Only a minority of weirdos jogged or performed all manner of violent exercise. Aerobics wasn't even a word. Adidas and Nikes predecessors were called sneakers, and a diet was an annoyance written on a piece of white paper in my fat doctor's office.

Do whatever makes you feel good. So many choices exist. I can't presume to propose a regimen for you. Whatever you choose, try to include your husband. It will make you feel heroic, useful and definitely more moral. Some of us need that. If you choose to go it alone, pick something that's fun and challenging. Men love challenging forms of exercise. Racquetball and weightlifting are marvelous body shapers and also good for body watching, body picking and body playing. Try this: visit a thin medical man for a complete physical and treadmill EKG before embarking on a rigorous course of physical fitness. Cheating is fun but hardly worth a coronary before you have a chance to participate. Who knows? One of us might even win a Gold Medal at the Senior Olympics or complete the Boston Marathon. All this good stuff from wanting a strange piece of ass. Shoot for the moon, ladies. There are so many rainbows to catch.

"What happens if he dies naked?"

CHAPTER 7

Locations

Now I lay me down to sleep.

I pray the Lord my soul to keep.

If I should die before I wake,

Let it be in my own bed.

A slight variation of the Bedtime Prayer, not meant to be sacrilegious.

I felt this fear for as long as I've been cheating, and I doubt that it will ever disappear. It is, however, not as strong today because I now realize you cannot cover every bet, and as a gambler in life I must accept some situations. I also realize that the chances of this ever happening are rare indeed. Many women tell me this disaster terrifies them so much it keeps them from realizing their heart's desire.

For days before a hotel tryst I would fantasize all sorts of sickness and death scenes. What happens if he dies naked? Do I dress him, leave him belly up—HELP! Is it my responsibility to stay with the body until his wife or family come to claim it? Sure it is, if I want to follow him into eternity. What do I do if he has a heart attack or some similar catastrophe? Ladies, why not visit your nearest Red Cross Center and spend just a few hours learning life-saving CPR (Cardio Pulmonary Resuscitation)? Not only is it good for the cheatee, it also benefits your entire family. I knew a lady who saved her lover from choking on a piece of meat using the Heimlich maneuver, then saved her husband from a coronary with CPR in the same month. I see her as a heroine and a smart one at that. I don't believe I could leave a man or any other human being on the brink of death to save my ass, so a little ER type information may definitely prove valuable. Again, you are prepared, minimizing your "get caught ratio."

If, on the other hand, you try everything humanly possible and he dies, get the hell out. Don't feel guilty. You didn't kill him. It's not a hit and run, and you will cause more grief by staying than if you split. You want to send flowers? Fine, but don't sign the card unless he's a member of your social set, in which case the wreath comes from you and your husband. This may strike you as maudlin, but I felt no stone should be left unturned, no matter how unpleasant.

What happens if it's you? The ultimate fear. Dying in disgrace. At least you won't have to worry about alibis. I thought about discussing this situation with my bed partners to alleviate my fears. I tried a few times and wound up upsetting the men I dallied with. They don't want to hear this. It's too frightening for the poor dears. Most men, lacking the maternal instincts genetics blessed us with, don't like to think about sickness and death. Which doesn't imply that we like it; we are programmed to deal with it. Our generation produced mommies and daddies with well-defined job descriptions. He worries about work, we worry about families. We haven't come that far from the Stone Age in that area. Some younger people of today are beginning to swap identities and share feelings. They welcome unisex in fashion and living situations, and it's terrific. It's the rare fifty- or sixty-year-old man, however, who can adapt to this concept. Besides, men make lousy patients and worse nurses. I did meet a man once who seemed genuinely interested in my thoughts on the matter until I discovered he was a borderline necrophiliac and was getting turned on by the whole gruesome business. An untimely demise is a chance you take, but the odds of it ever happening are almost nonexistent.

If you become seriously ill, call the desk and go straight to the hospital. With any luck, you'll be unconscious so no one will expect explanations until you recover. By then, your worried loved ones will be so grateful you're breathing, they'll believe the lie you relate no matter how ludicrous. People usually believe things that make them feel good. I'm sure your husband wants to feel better than he felt when you were critical. He's tired and hoping he can put the entire incident behind him so he can resume working with a clear mind and worry about his business instead of yours.

Location is everything in real estate and cheating. You want the best possible value when you buy a house; you want the same thing when you gamble with your future. Motels are the worst possible places for an affair. They project a sleazy image when you slink in alone, rather than checking in with the hubby, baby and assorted luggage. They also offer no alibis. If someone catches you in a motel or sees you arrive and exit, there's only one reason you're there. If motels provide the only nearby sleeping arrangements, I suggest you drive a few miles and find a hotel. Their restaurants or coffee shops give you at least a reason for visiting. A business lunch, meeting a friend for a bite, and if it has a bar, so much the better. That gives you two options. A food excuse, or "I stopped in for a drink." The more brazen among you can even meet the gentlemen at the bar and enjoy romantic foreplay as long as it's not above the table. You might even need a calm-me-down drink before going up to the room, and if someone spots you, hotel bars are better than corner saloons. Also much safer.

I came across a situation with a male friend, one-half of a married pair in our social circle. For what follows, remember you learned at the beginning of this book that you should not tell anyone about your interludes. I pretty much always knew that women were dangerous, but I couldn't let this particular opportunity pass me by, so I decided, why not take a chance with a man we will call Gerald?

It was rumored that Gerald rents an apartment in town. Nothing fancy, but convenient for private trysts. We suspected marital problems plagued him because of his fights with his wife at almost every social function they attended. So I approach him one evening at a barbecue with a mutually beneficial, viable proposition. I knew that his business was not going well. In his present financial crisis, I reason that sharing the burden of apartment renting with a neophyte philanderer, who couldn't afford one of her own, might interest him.

Poor Gerald, his ashen complexion at that moment made him look like a dead duck ready for the main course at dinner.

"How did you find out?" he asks in a low whine that must have driven his wife crazy.

I counter with, "I'm not a stool pigeon." I thought that would enhance my credibility as a closed-mouthed, part-time roommate.

"Gerald, just think of me as one of the boys. You lend them your key gratis; I'm willing to pay half the rent."

Gerald, visibly shaken, seems traumatized by what he perceives as sci fi women in our present society, versus the good-girl, bad-girl people he grew up with in Brooklyn. My businesslike approach catches him off guard because he should have denied access to any and all rooms he uses for extramarital affairs. He obviously had never read a book like this. I also, not knowing a tenth of what I know now, should have backed off. If taken prisoner, he would have given much more than name, rank and serial number.

I continued pointing out how simply we could communicate without suspicious phone calls and codes. We see each other all the time, we know each other's habits, and neither one of us wants to get caught, which would facilitate each protecting the other's interests.

"After all, Gerald, we are good friends," I declared.

His desperation over losing total control of the place brings him to a decision he feels is catastrophic. While he sullenly places a key in my hand during a break at a bridge game, Gerald rattles off a multitude of reasons for not giving me what he feels he is forced to give me. Gerald is laying a guilt trip on me in that same whiny voice, making me wonder if he's paying rent on an always empty flat. This is not a sexy, attractive picture. I had never seen Gerald in this light before, dim and dull.

Our first unpleasant encounter occurs over the décor. I can't tryst comfortably in a tacky, colorless apartment. Over much protesting from Gerald, who loves what he calls sensual modern, I start driving him crazy with frilly curtains, geraniums, needlepoint pillows, ballerina prints and a pink and white bedroom. More of Gerald's protests pour in, with him feeling trapped in an apartment that looks like the home he is running from, plus the fear that his ladies will think him more of a pansy than a sex object. Neither of us could tell our future visitors about the other. We agreed on that point before I began the great remodel. I didn't want an unhappy Gerald, but I was born to decorate and I haunted garage sales, never before having a reason to buy in quantity. Again, I was just acting out the role I knew.

A long-time housewife like me enjoys her routines and habits. The bird always feathers her nest before she lays her eggs. My mind starts straying off men and onto chintz. Much to my surprise, Gerald attracts a steady clientele that he staggers between my painting and laying of linoleum. Suddenly he's actually accommodating now that he finds a compassionate ear for his chronic moaning. In retrospect, I realize now that if you put me in any domestic situation, as if by remote control I react like a wife. Many trained domestic engineers over the age of thirty-five share this neurotic quirk of mine. Even with my college degree and ten thousand hobbies, my first instinct remains lady of the day rather than lady of the evening.

As the weeks progress, our relationship begins deteriorating. I become less receptive to his sniveling descriptions of miserable encounters of the female kind. His general sloppiness doesn't help matters. He in turn finds my intense neatness and constant "jabbering," as he calls it, unbearable. I complain about the dirty underwear of both genders piling higher and higher, tons of laundry unattended, messy bathroom hygiene, and the beginnings of his forgetfulness about our schedules. On one occasion, I am sent racing into the nearest closet, paint roller in hand, as he escorts his newest conquest into the lair. I am now compulsively cleaning two households, with the tryst being the most difficult of the two. The entire debacle transforms me into a monumental nag.

My husband notices my odd behavior; it ranges from manic excitement whenever I contemplate my first usage of the pink and white room to general lethargy from the chores both Gerald and my husband shirk.

I discuss with Gerald the difficulty factor in living dual lives. He offers absolutely no sound advice while continuously defying the odds of detection because of his laziness. I may be a romantic, but I am also a realist, so I take on the added burden of covering Gerald's tracks. If one rat gets trapped, I decide, they both go down with the sinking apartment.

As you might imagine, this arrangement proves unacceptable to both of us. Gerald holds a lease but a sublet is easy due to my neurotic, yet rather brilliant decorating.

Fooling around cannot be a full-time job. Your family, if you wish to stay with it successfully, should always remain your first concern. Visit his house, a hotel, the backseat of a car if you must. Do not attempt two households. Most of us, if we are honest with ourselves, barely do one properly.

Remember the baggy-eyed female boozer I spoke of in an earlier chapter? "I did it in a water cave in Greece on a rock with only my swim fins on," she told me. "At forty-eight years of age I did it on a crowded beach under a blanket with an underaged ice cream vendor. I've done it on the Staten Island Ferry while everyone was staring at the New York skyline and in a ferris wheel at a county fair."

Many men utilize their offices, unattached friends' apartments, and business trips. If you're lucky, you'll meet one of them. If you're even luckier, you'll stretch your imagination like the boozer, using your innate common sense, and discover a place in time you will never forget.

"In my home, I was a sofa, bought, paid for and owned."

CHAPTER 8
Why Me?

Many writers give other writers their material to critique. I gave this manuscript, half finished, to "Harold" and "Barbara." I trust these people will keep my story confidential. Harold saw a lot of anger. He felt I came down too hard on the male population and my revelations to the female masses were dangerous to the American way of life with its peculiar checks and balances that keep women out of the male domain.

"You are, after all, wives and mothers, and are needed in that capacity," Harold said.

He never mentioned the words "rewarded emotionally," "cherished" or "appreciated." Barbara, a basically conservative, upper middle-class married lady in her early fifties, said, "Where were you when I needed you?"

Women have been particularly liberated in many areas but not sexually in the true sense of the word. I mentioned this fact in an earlier chapter, but let me stress it again. The gay population has more sexual freedom than we do.

Like "Mother, the flag and apple pie," the image that keeps the double standard alive and well will continue for many generations, if not forever. Not everyone you know will admonish or chastise you if you get caught but most will, of both sexes.

Barbara, unhappily married for many years, said, "At one time in my life I would have considered outside sex. Divorce was out of the question for a variety of reasons. But if someone had given me even the slightest push, guided or motivated me at that time in my life, I would have done it and not felt cheated by life as I do now."

Odd, isn't it, that she felt cheated by not cheating? She lacked romantic memories. Nothing to fall back on or dream of when her world seemed hopeless and lonely. We are like that, all of us, no matter how tough or responsible. We need our fantasies.

I have taken small, inconsequential meetings with men and blown them out of proportion into Rhett Butler and Scarlett O'Hara at Tara when I felt unattractive and unimportant in my married life, which was most of the time.

I told Barbara it was not too late for her, but I knew it was. For some of us, life never stops evolving. For others, emotional death comes long before physical death, and all the heart massage in the world can never bring them back; the bitter, teary-eyed ladies of this world who stop trying, who tire of searching for something they think is a million light years away, if it exists at all.

I'm sure some of you will make a negative character judgment on what I've been doing with my life, but don't judge too harshly. I wish I could tell you I was battered, bruised and physically deformed from all the muscle my first husband put on me. I'm not. I am, however, like many of you, all those things emotionally and more.

To the outside world I was a person with humor, looks and style. In my home I was a sofa, bought, paid for and owned. He sat on me, figuratively speaking, got up and left at will, fluffed me up after his ass was off me, and scuffed my Queen Anne legs when he tripped over me, with no apology. He praised my worth when people complimented my antique value, never talking directly at the sofa. After all, he wasn't crazy. Who talks to furniture? He punched my pillows when he was angry at his business or the kids, and put his feet up on my brocade fabric when he wanted to relax. He took me out on rare occasions, when he wanted to show off his worth, and I suspect from the indelicate and infrequent way he pounced on my stuffing that he visited other pieces.

I won't bore you with trivial stories about the two of us. I'm sure you've heard them before from most of your friends, including the universal complaint from a big segment of the wifely population: "He treats me like a stick of furniture.

There can be nothing more demeaning to a gentle soul than being ignored, thereby excising personal value in the most personal of relationships. I gave one thousand percent to my mate during our time together, and he gave me less effort than he puts into his golf game. In many cases we ladies are but a cog in the wheel of their lives, and when we finally break loose—watch that wheel go out of control. Then they start their "I gave her everything" routine and actually believe it. Most of us middle-aged babies remain buried in the rompers our husbands nailed to our bottoms. Why did I live in this vacuum?

As I chronicle my life and read about my actions and my capabilities, I find more courage to grow up. As I said before, the media exerts a strong influence in all our lives, and the oldest form of media, the printed word, rates as the strongest. If I hadn't left the marriage I would have sought remuneration for all the jobs I did well in the form of pleasure, without caring who paid me as long as I collected my check from someone who knew my worth.

Many things are better left unsaid. I would never have confronted my husband as long as we were together with my suspicions of his infidelity. He would probably have told me it was none of my business and then confessed. My God, how men love baring their souls and cleansing their minds, and, as good mommies, we let them. That's the tape men and women play over and over again. In the media, TV and movies the men confess with a tear and a croaking whine or, worse, with pride, and we, after the initial shock breaks our hearts, open our earth-mother arms and soothe their guilt-ridden egos. How many times have you seen the roles reversed in the media or in real life? In the rare instances when it does happen, the only way the cheating women are taken back is by paying some awful kind of penance. What's more, they must portray saintly ladies from the outset, and the men who accept their mortal sins come across as weak, useless morons.

In real life, and I use the term "real" with some reservation, men can't allow us to capitalize on their sins. The world isn't set up that way, but it will if I get my way. Women generate the power on this planet. When we finally realize just how much clout we possess, I hope we use it more judiciously than the men of the past. We shall temper power with mercy, but not too much unless it's deserved. Remember that lady who holds the Scales of Justice, the logo of the law. Even she is blindfolded, as important as she is. Take off your

73

blindfolds and maneuver yourselves through life without walking into walls. It's just too painful stubbing your toe every time you stop crawling with your teething ring stuck in your mouth, silencing you. Instead, start walking with a steady gait.

Why do I feel someone will assassinate me or hang me for treason when our other halves read this rather long memo from the office of the lady who has finally broken their code?

"My prince can be your frog."

CHAPTER 9

Who Do You Do It With?

Since I am primarily concerned with heterosexual relationships, the obvious answer to this question is—MEN.

Men are wonderful people. Most of my dearest friends are men. They seem blessed with marvelous friendship qualities. They listen, advise, and compliment me when I deserve it. They rattle my cage with a basic no-nonsense honesty I don't find in their female counterparts. I like their earthy humor, their disdain of female gossip, and the way they reach the heart of things without verbal squirming and backbiting. Most of the time they may be sons-of-bitches in business with their own kind, but as friends they are unparalleled. The competitive faction in a male-female-relationship of the friendly kind is nonexistent.

This is what I have found in all my stand-up situations with men. As soon as you change the anatomical position to supine, or "Let's lie down for a few hours," everything changes. I'm not saying always, but I feel the majority of people manifest peculiar behavior after they shed their inhibitions and clothes. This is our first category of men. The ones we stand shoulder to shoulder with and the ones we lie on, so to speak.

Fabulous Freddie, that light-hearted, mellow, considerate person you play softball with on Sundays, will probably be a different Freddie after the softball becomes hardball. He may not lose his peachy personality traits, or he may. But you can bet on new ones emerging after sex. When you unlock the mystery of you and Freddie below the waist, an almost immediate unlocking of you and Freddie in the head occurs. Physical intimacy breeds emotional intimacy, and if both of you are reasonably stable, the two of you may experience growth with a possible strengthening of the friendship. It won't remain the same but it can be better. However, if one or both of you fall into what I call the present universal state of mind—namely, neurotic—things can become weird. Suddenly, you may experience jealousy, fear, rejection, tension, whining, possessiveness and fighting. There goes the friendship for the sake of a possible great lay. Is it worth it? I don't think so. You take a calculated risk with a good friend. If it goes awry, maybe you can patch it up, but it will never be the same. If your life is such that you cannot go outside your social group to fornicate, you would be wise to choose a marginal friend. Really special friends are hard to come by.

Now, about enemies... We discussed friends, both good and marginal. Now all that is left in this first and broad category of men is enemies. If your mind needs the convoluted, miserable stimulation associated with guerrilla fighting, you'd be safer in many jungles in exotic places like Central America. A rebel fighter in El Salvador with a machine gun in hand and grenades in her teeth would have an easier time than a lady who would try seducing a gentleman who loathes her. Don't do it.

Let's cover the negative stuff early on in this chapter. Put off limits the men who seem firmly attached to your lady friends, whether by marriage or a living arrangement. Not only is it bad taste hitting on them, it is also dangerous. If they make the first move, the same moral judgment applies. If you are single and their relationship looks shaky, I'd say, "Go for it." But if you are single, you would be reading another book. Anyway, it's just too close to home.

I experienced this problem twice. One husband, persistent devil he, almost scored. He nearly won me over with his bullshit philosophy—not because I'm stupid, but because I longed for the tasty morsel. His belief? The most obvious affair, right out where everyone could see it, would escape notice. We could sneak around in private, and continue being openly affectionate in public the same as before. The human animal, unless he's logged ten years of method acting, can't pull that off. It's also very wearing on the psyche. Once you touch lying down, the stand-up act changes. The peck on the cheek becomes more lingering. The eye contact sparks more fervor. As the Harlequin romance says, "The flames rise within the loins as they touch across a crowded room." Obvious becomes quite obvious to Harriet, who tells Ethel, and so on until your hubby hears the news.

Let's assume you have three or four close female friends. Chances are at least two of them are divorced or separated. Most divorced couples communicate with each other on financial matters or about child visitation details. Even if these factors don't exist, they probably take time despising each other on the telephone or in person. A divorce often may turn ugly, and years go by before old grudges disappear, if ever. If you choose one of these men, he could use you as a lethal left hook in one of their main events. If, however, the man was once attached to a lady you rarely see, the odds are more in your favor. If she lives in another city or country, he might be a safe bet.

I have a single friend who captures more attention on freeways and busy city streets than Mario Andretti. She is stunning and crazy. If I make a dinner date with her, she'll arrive with one of her Mercedes specials fifty percent of the time. How? She's driving alone toward the restaurant, stops for a light, looks left and falls in love. She knows this man for the time it takes driving to the restaurant from whatever point on the map she picked him up. That's usually twenty minutes. We three eat dinner, he picks up the check, and off they go. I tell her, "It's a dangerous business, and Jack the Ripper's illegitimate, deranged great-grandson might enjoy driving an expensive foreign car this year." She laughs.

The casual pickup is fine; so is the dinner in a crowded restaurant. The male always arrives in his own car. That tête-a-tête might furnish a morale boost for you. It's the going to your place that's too chancy. Make a date and see him again if you like him. Have a drink or lunch. Go anywhere with people in attendance at least until you know what he's all about. Married women must worry not only about their physical safety but also about their matrimonial safety. If he's unstable or non caring about your mental welfare, you'll know it in time. This really applies to any pickup. It might happen while you're shopping, in a bar, wherever you might be for short periods of time. I don't care how he turns you on or how charming he is or how beautifully turned out he may be. Cross your legs, take a cold shower, and wait.

Coast-to-coast pickups are safer. I consider airplanes one of the best male supermarkets in existence. If you fly, choose a time when businessmen take to the sky. The longer the flight the better. However, don't do it in the john. Take time to interrogate gently. If you like what you see, land safely, deplane and disrobe.

As long as we're discussing pickups in general, there is always the chance that you might meet someone who knows your husband. We live in a small world. Before you become sexually suggestive, do a little business-, geographic- and name-probing. Use your real name when you meet. After all, you are not committing a crime in the beginning of the verbal stage. During this strictly friendly stage, give true information about yourself. Tell him you're married and pass lightly over what your husband does for a living. Don't even mention the company, but if he comes back with, "I'm in the same field," and it's a small field, I wouldn't continue the conversation beyond au revoir. If it's a big industry like insurance, you ask the questions. Men love talking about their work, and he'll take your interest as a sign of real caring. If he's married, his wife probably never makes inquiries of this nature, and you make points. If he's married and as careful as you are, you'll probably engage in an all-question and no-answer conversation on both sides. Take this as a good sign and pursue it further. He's playing if safe, and take his wariness as a sign he's smart. The best kind of playmate.

Let's talk about money. We are all in this for different reasons. If it's only romance or animal sex, money counts for little unless you live in the upper financial stratum of society, in which case you might forgo a wicked whackado with a welder. If you regularly quaff Dom Perignon, Gallo Chablis could give you a monumental headache and ruin the nooner. It's been my experience that people usually travel in their own class anyway, even if it's just a hotel visit. Just as many stockbrokers fool around as telephone linemen.

Let's consider the three financial categories: 1) Mega bucks; 2) Almost broke or the middle class; 3) Candidates for debtor's prison. You'll probably pop for booze and bed for the debtors. Not my preference, but if you possess lots of green and prefer spending it on him in lieu of cars, caviar and clothes, it's your choice.

Most of you probably encounter the middle income type. This category contains a lot of people in lower, middle and upper middle classes. Cheating is not cheap. Your joint expense sheet includes places such as hotels, lunches, dinners, drinks, transportation, and, on your side, clothes and cosmetics. Women invariably feel they must adorn their bodies with new raiment for the new guy on the block. For the rest of the items, going dutch or sharing the expense might prove necessary if it's a long affair. Usually, the man springs for the whole shebang at the beginning. He can't help it. He's been programmed by society. But if it continues for weeks or months and he receives orthodontist bills for little Tildy, or his Toyota breaks down periodically, he will apprise you of his money problems. The longer you know each other and the closer you snuggle, the more problems you will share. A long affair resembles a marriage. The good news? You can dash home instead of seeing a lawyer when you don't like the scene.

Many people of both genders feel they must regale their lovers with life stories almost immediately after consummating their lust. This often shortens an affair because one or both of the consenting parties prefer "no news is good news" to hearing about bad times in downtown Dubuque just after they've reached orgasm.

Helping with the bills will be more difficult. Some of us ladies lack control of the checkbook, so tapping the household money could tip off the family when you present spaghetti fifty different ways in as many days. This puts the burden on the man. You'll experience fewer problems if you find one who can afford to cheat, rents his own apartment or will go into debt because he's embarrassed about admitting his financial shortcomings. If you keep indulging in short affairs, and learned something from my mistake with the baritone in an earlier chapter, you should avoid virtually all mishaps.

I will mention physical appearance in passing. Chemistry affects all of us in different ways. My prince can be your frog. I don't imagine many of us would turn down a Tom Selleck look-alike unless he's a total asshole—and even then, maybe once...However, like us, most men don't resemble movie stars, so latch onto whatever looks good.

The mind is important; not necessarily education per se, but how your personalities meld. If you're fighting with your husband you wouldn't want World War III with a stranger. Mental stimulation is closely related to sexual stimulation. The best kind of lovemaking starts with a sentence. Good looks fall by the wayside if the Adonis needs help operating an elevator. If, however, you are one of those busy women in the work force who contends with more than enough mental nonsense, the dumb jerk may be just what you require. How long have men been referring to the dumb blonde with big tits and no brains? She's good for a bang. Well, high-powered lady executives, bang away if you find a gorgeous dumb blond fellow with an organ suited for a fabulous fugue. Please remember, I am not condoning or making any sort of judgments; I am merely presenting you with the facts accumulated in my research. There is no wrong or right, except for the few times I have committed myself to a preference. Not hurting anyone is the key, and if you take care and remain prudent, such should be the case. If you get hurt, it's the price you pay for the gamble you took. By exercising extra caution, that shouldn't happen either.

Professional bullshitters provide great fun. They'll regale you with amusing stories and anecdotes, real or imagined. They will compliment your looks, mind, and anything else that brings your focus completely on them. It can't hurt as long as you keep the bullshit in its proper perspective and don't start believing his rave reviews. These guys can really make your husband look pale in comparison. If your husband of long standing still tells you, "Your body drives me wild with passion," or "Your magnificent face is with me always, so beautiful and perfect," or "You make Sophia Loren look like a toad," you're truly blessed.

Try and remember, no matter your degree of loveliness, the new man will spout poetry within his limitations and exaggerate a bit. Even if he absolutely believes everything he says, he still does not take responsibility for you or hear you snore. He doesn't see the pitiful mess that is you when the flu strikes or peer in horror after you cleaned a three-bedroom house in the summer without air conditioning at the height of the worst hot spell in thirty years.

It's really amazing how the most brilliant professor or businessman can make earth-shattering decisions that benefit mankind in the most positive way, but can't pay his wife a single compliment. If he only knew by giving her two or three compliments she's his forever. He can work doggedly on one experiment in minute detail, but can't notice the ten pounds you lost. Women commit these same errors, but I tend to think not as much as men. Anyway, this book is about our business.

Men who ignite my fire usually focus more on mental stimulation than physical. I often wonder if the physical happens as a byproduct of the mental. Making love offers so many levels, and for each of us the first step toward the bedroom will differ. Men who don't make me laugh or prod my thinking process seldom turn me on. I love the verbal fencing. He must talk me into bed. This has nothing to do with formal education and everything to do with personality.

All of us will relish at least one encounter that brings a smile to our lips and warms our souls long after the gentleman departs from our lives. We will possess no tangible reminders of him because we're too clever for memento keeping. I'll bet that, whoever he is, his style and not his physical attributes made him special.

People indulging in affairs spend little time together, so they talk about common interests without much doing. It's nice when you share things you both like but do not regard as too important. So casual ties give you such a broad range of men from which to choose. You do not seek a permanent partner. If you did, then stamp collecting, if that's your major passion, would be a prime prerequisite. We can pass over hobbies in common rather quickly. If you find a mutual interest, so much the better. If not, no great loss. You can meet men who do totally foreign things and benefit from their sharing. This kind of educational process proves quite enriching. I know that cheating, used as a learning tool, must seem a bit far-fetched, but then, so were computers a few years ago.

Young men make better lovers. A rather stunning statement, but one I regard as true. Don't take this, however, as a signal; resist rushing to the nearest schoolyard and grabbing a lad during recess. "Young" represents not only a state of physical being but also an attitude. It's the ability for spontaneity and dreaming dreams as yet unfulfilled that you approach with positive vigor. "Young" is necking in a car, giggling in bed and on one foot wearing a mitten with the painted face of a puppet your lover hears and sees upon awakening. "Young" is crying unashamedly and speaking real feelings with little pretense and lots of honesty. "Young" is what we all were but most have forgotten because society tells us that growing up makes you cynical, cautious and defensive.

I know some men in their fifties and up who qualify as young, but not many. The others learned their growing-up lessons too well. I'm not implying that women remain unafflicted as well. They don't. Women, however, possess the knack of reaching back, given the right environment, and relearning the magic of prom night. Women spend much of their lives with their children, the Easter Bunny and Santa Claus. Thus they retain more qualities from childhood days than their counterparts.

If you meet the rare man who can be both child and grown-up in appropriate situations, then congratulations on finding the best of all men. Good luck. If I faced a choice between a mostly grown-up man who knew all the best wines and had traveled the globe three times or a hometown kind of man who drinks beer but arrives at our rendezvous with an arrow drawn on his stomach in glowy stuff with my name on it that only shows up in the dark, pointing at his erection—no contest. This artistic tour de force actually happened to me some years ago. A great deal of thought went into that gift, and lots of laughter erupted when the lamp went out.

I spent some time with a fella twelve years my junior. We shared little in common except humanity. His clear, bright eyes were not clouded with suspicion and sadness. Young men haven't yet confronted excessive abuse by ladies or the world in general. What little abuse they have undergone in love relationships hasn't made chronic scars.

I told him about cruises and fine restaurants, and he spoke of destinations and how he knew he would reach them. He told me, "I can't" wasn't an acceptable phrase. He said I was beautiful. He believed that age meant nothing if two people fit well together. I thought then how unfair life could be because I knew the outcome of this fairy tale and he didn't. I was, after all, "grown up." How unfair for both of us. I was the older one but he was the teacher. We made love because he had not yet learned nor could he stomach a feelingless fuck on a regular basis. How many of us lived with F.F. for years, never dreaming that we could enjoy the other kind again.

I know it's unfair comparing this young man with my husband. I tried resisting because I knew I lacked the courage to leave my secure life for the constant surprises and possible failure in the single world. I was all grown up and very frightened. I brought some of his contagious attitude home to my family. It made a marvelous impact on the kids and a lesser one on my husband. I became a different wife and mommy, but more important, I became a different individual. This was something for me, and I never let go of it. I had become a little less grown up, and I thank him for that.

The kind of joy I experienced from this affair makes it premier on my list of life experiences. He also convinced me that I make a list of all the things I want to do while I inhabit planet Earth. I've achieved about forty percent of them to date. Many of my do's are modest in nature, some are frivolous, and one or two downright outrageous. He's right, you know. "I can't" only exists if you allow it. Sure, you'll encounter toughies, some real bitches, but so far, not one "I can't."

This personal experience was an affair of the spirit primarily and sexual in nature secondarily. If you find both elements in one encounter and each one bristles the hairs on your neck whenever you meet, then you have found the best of all affairs—and the beginning of trouble. It's difficult to leave such a man.

Time in the sack certainly improves techniques of lovemaking. The longer you're at it, the more time there is, through trial and error, for discovering all the right moves. Sometimes, if you're at it too long, the moves become mechanical and habitual, leading to a yawning partner who reads the evening paper while you moan halfheartedly at precisely 11:06 p.m. What about making love on the kitchen sink or the back seat of your Volkswagen, because you feel like it and not because it's Wednesday? Younger men usually forgo mechanical technique. They're exploring all forms of life with so many surprises and no apparent schedule.

You could time many of the older men I've known like a three-minute egg. They start with a kiss on the mouth, down the neck to the breast. Open wide and it's over. Even the spread eagle marathoner, with a stop watch in his head, times for twenty-six miles. I half expected some of them to wear one around their necks, blow a whistle, push the button, "On your mark…"

I met a charming gentleman playing tennis. We lunched several times and he enchanted me with his sophistication, humor and gentleness. When I finally arrived at his home, a modest bungalow at the beach, my heart pounded with anticipation. Corny as this sounds, I heard it thumping.

We sipped wine on the patio, indulged in heavy petting in the living room, and he actually carried me into the bedroom. Eat your heart out, Ava Gardner, I thought, as we landed on the bed. We disrobed in the dark room, he nibbled on my ear, and I saw stars.

Unfortunately, they were painted on his ceiling. Lights, camera, action. The geezer considered himself a reincarnated C.B. DeMille.

Spotlights glared. Suddenly I saw huge, velvet-framed tigers with bared fangs on the wall. A fiercely menacing Doberman sat on his haunches. He was stuffed. Then the red furniture caught my eye. Mirrors everywhere, and a large TV screen overflowed with ladies devouring a humongous set of male genitals. Honestly, I couldn't move. I knew the fool wasn't dangerous; I was simply overwhelmed. He operated vibrators plugged in on each side of the bed, and bragged about a combination kitchen-bathroom display on the oversized nightstand. We had our choice of whipped cream, Vaseline, passion oils, flavored joy gels and chocolate syrup. When the cold whipped cream hit my crotch, I thought, "You're February's flavor of the month," and I came to life.

An intensely heated discussion ensued while I tried dressing, putting my leg into my bra strap. This was his act, he proclaimed, "Seedy burlesque," I answered, slightly disoriented. He purred with great pride about the other ladies' multiple orgasms on the set. He firmly believed, and his years of research proved, that he owned the ultimate sex room and nothing would be changed. "If you can't appreciate the work and money I've put into this project, you must be frigid," he shouted. I tried telling him that we all had dissimilar tastes and what works for one could turn off another. He wasn't buying it. He handed me my purse with a look of utter disdain and showed me the door. This, my dear ladies, represents an intolerable degree of degradation. This guy was very, very old.

Yet, some of you might find this environment a turn-on, and I understand that. I couldn't, however, abide his inflexibility, insensitivity, disconcern for my preferences, and his deadpan expression when I fastened my bra around my hips and pulled my panties over my head. This fool had overdone his sack time. On the way out I noticed the fleas in his carpet practicing for the next Olympic high hurdles. The dog must have been newly stuffed.

If you find yourselves in uncomfortable situations, speak up, then scat. Don't feel you must stay to avoid a scene or keep from hurting his feelings. Remember, a fling provides pleasure, not toil. A friend of mine, despite a bad back, allowed herself to be laid on top of a grand piano and spent two agonizing months in a brace. The piano top, it seemed, was the only place he could play his instrument. His fetish probably provided the wherewithal for ten chiropractors early retirement.

If you think these two stories border on the twilight zone, you're right. If, however, you explore often enough, the odds of this kind of outer limits experience increase markedly. The most conservative bank teller by day may metamorphose into the kinkiest freak at dusk. All the rules and mores of society plummet right down the toilet when he drops his shorts. This is not the norm, but you can't escape meeting a couple of whackos sooner or later. That sense of humor I mentioned earlier becomes your best defense in these moments of crisis. You'll experience an overpowering, almost violent urge to tell someone what took place. How do you keep such juicy gossip a secret? You just witnessed the neighborhood butcher in a pink tutu with matching tights and garter belt. This is not easily contained. You know the consequences of blabbing this one while visiting a friend. You may as well stuff an apple in your mouth and plop down as his Hawaiian luau display. "My own mother couldn't keep this quiet," you tell yourself, which proves that bizarre encounters are the most dangerous. Rest assured the butcher remains discreet even if you split your sides laughing and he hates you. The last thing he wants is notoriety. Rate him as the safest affair you'll ever experience, if you control your tongue.

Older men tell many stories. As I listen, I often feel that it's eleven o'clock news time. Misery, mayhem and other assorted tales of wretched violence fill the air. Women complain to women. Men complain to any ear that will bend, including mine. I reeled from lamentations about ex-wives, alimony, disease, pestilence, kiddie problems, work-related disasters, monetary depressions, old girlfriends, enlarged prostates, broken dentures, and hemorrhoids. Eight million stories in the naked city and each guy knows at least six mil. God, how they suffer in their Bally shoes and Jaguars. They want us beaming, bright and chipper, a happy face at cocktail time. How vivacious can one be after an in-depth discussion of Preparation H?

Younger men talk about sailing, surfing, how lovely your hair looks, and their Labrador retrievers. If they discuss their problems, it's usually in a positive manner. They remain unaware of the fact that women often substitute as crying towels. Most of them don't even know that some women become doormats. If they like spending time with you, it's time well spent. They approach you as a friend. They sometimes revere you, so don't abuse it. Never feel guilty about it, and remember every moment. It's a wonderful memory you can recall when hubby passes gas in bed after spending most of the evening complaining about his ex-wife, alimony payments, rotten kids, his boss, your financial extravagance, and his hemorrhoids.

"Do not float through your daily mundane chores like a soppy cocker spaniel."

CHAPTER 10
Falling in Love

We all do it, ladies; some of us once a year, others every other day. We make falling in love our national pastime, giving the men baseball and football. It's a lot more dangerous than a full-on tackle from a gorilla with a thirty-inch neck. The entire Rams defensive line couldn't cause more damage than one female in love with someone other than her husband.

Love? It can get you caught. "They say that falling in love is wonderful. It's wonderful, so they say." that's right, whoever they are. I can't put it down. I can't tell you, "Avoid love." I've done it myself in varying degrees. I can only tell you: recognize the symptoms as they appear. Take the proper medication and control the disease as best you can. Do not float through your daily mundane chores like a soppy cocker spaniel after appearing for years on wash day like a snappy terrier.

If you're one of those rare women who glides through life on cloud nine devoid of menstrual-like misery moods ninety percent of the time, you've got it made. No one will know the difference. You're in the minority. Most of us married ladies snarl quite a bit. We'd startle those around us by smiling all the time.

Remember falling in love? You think only of him. Daisies and daffodils blanket the world. The rain holds a new meaning. You stop noticing the kinds' messy rooms. You ignore all eight hundred of your husband's faults. You stare a lot. You can't remember anger as a state of mind. You and Hal rejoice in your own little gorgeous world, while you continue living in husband Herbie's house.

Sorry. You can't do this successfully. Family and friends will accuse you of raging schizophrenia. When they find out you're not nuts, you're caught. You cannot indulge yourselves in childlike fantasies out in the open in view of everyone. Instead, play the role of a closet cocker spaniel if you want to stay married. Feelings of warmth and love certainly make you a different person. Even if you make a valiant containment attempt, people will still notice a change. If you make no attempt to disguise your feelings, you're a goner. Some husbands, of course, wouldn't notice if you grew an extra nose. If this sounds familiar, enjoy yourselves. You deserve it.

Your friends will probably see the change first. Don't let them wring it out of you. Believe me, they will try, first with compliments, then with concern for your health. They will use every female trick to get the story. They recognize the ailment, but they can't prove it if you keep quiet.

So much of this advice is plain common sense, but few women exhibit any sense at all when they're stricken. They absolutely believe they're keeping their emotions under wraps and conducting business as usual. I don't think so.

Songwriters say, "The look of love is in your eyes," and they're right again. Your facial contours actually change, depending on the depth of the feeling. Your eyes glow; wrinkles undergo a subtle smoothing out, and your body language changes. If you fall in love every Wednesday whether you need it or not, things remain pretty much the same. If you haven't been there for some time or do it seldom, be careful.

Mull this subject over before venturing into the world of cheating. "I want it all," some women declare. Well, it's not always possible. We can control feelings, depending on what's at stake. So you say, "What's the point of doing it if you can't feel it when you find it?" You can feel it within the boundaries of good sense. You don't see a lot of married men walking into walls when they cheat. "Oh, lady writer," you protest. "They're different." Only because society programmed them to act in appropriate ways. Appropriate for them. You must deprogram yourselves for your own good. You can feel love without a massive advertising campaign. It isn't necessary that you lose control in public proving to yourself and the world that you love. It's the media again. They show us that women in love swoon, faint, and become weak amoebas. Men become strong and function fabulously. Double horsepuckies. We should derive massive amounts of strength from such a positive emotion. Fainting and swooning went out with Garbo. This information pertains to the initial onslaught of love, which is usually associated with the beginnings of affairs.

My definition of love is whatever gives you butterflies and tingles. To some its physical or emotional or a combination of both, and it's really tough concealing the combo pack.

Some of you will fall in love and leave your husbands, and in some cases, many times. This sort of behavior destroys your credibility, and on your return you will probably pay dearly for it with guilt and harassment from the one you left. Some of you will fall and realize it's gone too far, necessitating a breakup. Or you may find a super relationship and keep it for as long as you can, living two lives with almost equal flair. Envy and imitate this kind of woman.

All right, you're in love. You're also getting away with it by being a sweetie with him and a wifey with hubby. Suddenly, the affair ends. Who cares what the reason is? The loss of love proves devastating whether you left or got dumped. Unfortunately, if you stay married, count on many endings. Avoid the word "future." If this all sounds so hard and cold. It is. It must, unless you find Mr. Right and feel the marriage needs dissolving. We all want happy endings and find almost none in a cheating relationship. Hiding love was one thing; hiding misery is another.

An ending or loss needs a mourning period, a real test of a woman's mettle. It's really difficult showing some semblance of normalcy when your heart is being torn out by the roots. I haven't yet met anyone who pulled this one off with great success. Grieving, difficult enough in private, becomes unbearable when you must care for the family and they intrude upon your grief without knowing the state of your misery. They laugh and want the chatter. They talk about fun stuff or aggravate you, and there's no escape. You're home. They insist you giggle with them. How dare they.

You can use many alibis for just such occasions. Menopause is a good one. If you're in your thirties, early menopause is rare, but it happens. Migraines work; so do backaches. Any sort of health problem will explain your erratic behavior. Visit the doctor if they insist. He can't prove you don't have these common maladies. By the time he's finished all the tests, you should be better. As time passes, the family will only note a minor mope after you see or hear something that reminds you of Hal. I've known some ladies who quit fooling around because of just such a situation. It's like falling off a horse, I believe. If you get back on immediately you can ride again without fear.

I use Hal as a composite. We all recall idyllic moments with at least one such fellow. When you think you have fallen in love with Hal, examine the emotion with careful scrutiny. You find little resemblance between cheating dating and unmarried dating. When you're free, there's time for exploring, discovery. Our kind of dating gives us little time to know Hal. Falling in love takes scads of time. Unless you enjoy at least two-hour dates every other day for a period of at least one year, how can you know the man? Love at first sight? Terrific, but hardly lasting.

I remember sudden lightning flashes only to find disappointing storms leading into wimpy summer showers

Let's suppose you're unhappy at home. Men you wouldn't consider suitable suitors if you were single begin looking good. You lack the time for cruising around, so you can't compare Hal with Homer or Heathcliff. Variety is missing. After being downgraded or ignored for so long, the first Hal who says something flattering achieves a stature all out of proportion. You're needy and hungry, and we all know that the worst time to shop for food is when you're hungry. You buy everything and stuff yourself, and eventually end up with a tummy ache. Sharpen your awareness of this hunger. It keeps you out of the junk food section and into gourmet goodies. Be selective just as if you were single. If you must fall in love, at least tumble with someone worthy of you.

My Hal brightened my life some time ago. He looked like Kermit the frog with a hormone problem. Very short. Also quite overweight. My husband was a looker. As it turned out, I really did feel love for this Hal. His dry and gentle humor blended with extraordinary, genuine kindness. Polished, yet down to earth, he could camp out like Grizzly Adams serving the finest champagne in tin cups and brilliantly explain the aurora borealis. He didn't know he looked like Kermit, and soon I didn't know it either. After three months, he became Cary Grant. A woman's eyes look from the soul. He gave me compliments I deserved and, when warranted, occasional criticism in a constructive manner. He became my friend and lover—a first for me till then.

Hal, though, became a problem. I wanted his companionship permanently. Before meeting him, I disliked going home. Now it was torture. I knew the kids would adore him. In retrospect, I recognize now the danger of leaving a marriage for another marriage without enough strength and capability of standing on your own two feet. I remained the same person who married Herbie. Toting all my neurotic crazies into the new relationship probably would have screwed it up.

Anyway, back to Hal. I was eighteen again, with all the appropriate symptoms, including a biggie—loss of appetite. Too bad, because Hal had bread, and I passed up some fine dinners shuttled into his home from the best restaurants in town. I also incurred blindness—one of the most critical symptoms of puppy love. I thought he saw me as Cleopatra, floating alone in superior majesty on his barge down the Nile. I overstuffed myself with this conceit.

I didn't need to see anyone else. Hal gave me everything I needed and more. When at home, I daydreamed about him constantly. Because we saw each other only once or twice a week for a few hours, we never fought. Who finds time for fighting or even discussing differences? Urgency permeates these kinds of affairs. You say something strip, screw, smoke and speak again for about fifteen minutes. Telephone time, which I deem crucial for two people discovering each other, was sparse. He conducted a booming business during the day when I could talk, and I reprised my role as wife and mother at night. So Hal became the perfect man. It's difficult pinpointing faults in a dream world.

The bottom line, using a current idiom, proved disastrous. When I finally declared my undying love, Harold reverted to Kermit. He had viewed me as a perfect woman because I made no demands. Kermie ranted and raved. Didn't I know he saw other women? Didn't I know he detested children? Did he ever actually even hint that he wanted something permanent? How dare I ruin his favorite two afternoons a week by being pushy and making him feel trapped. How dare I upset his stomach by fueling his cruel streak. You know, ladies, Kermie definitely scored some valid points here. I didn't see them at the time because of the hurt, but he connected. After a time, I took stock of the five-month affair and realized I really knew nothing.

My family and friends diagnosed me as terminally ill and resented my keeping it from them. In my misery, I let them believe it. For a month I looked like an embalmed zombie who forgot to hop in the box. I paraded my grief so everyone could see. What a putz, and oh so selfish. If I must suffer, I would inflict everyone around me.

I learned two lessons from this tormenting error in judgment and deed:

Some roundabout, subtle discussion reveals what a man thinks and feels.

Balance physical communicating with verbal communicating. Talk not only about the stars but how he stands on real issues as well. An affair can be very rewarding when the mix is romantic and real.

I use the word "real" often. Many of us avoid the real in these situations because of the overwhelming real at home. It's just too hazardous avoiding what's real in the man as well as yourself. We're running away from home when we escape the conjugal bed and desire Peter Pan plus The Nutcracker Suite. "The affair" becomes our escape, and we feel trapped and badly injured when we hit the dead end. It's not so bad if we know our options and the location of hairpin turns during the run. By knowing what's "real," we prepare ourselves for the inevitable end or stall it for a long time by not wearing crash helmets while racing around. Hal is not a mythical god devoid of human failings. Know the failings and bleed less. And if you must bleed, tie a tight tourniquet in public and loosen it in private. Your family shouldn't sit in the stands watching the accident happen. They travel freeways of their own.

"Crabs, those dreadful little creatures, crawl around your pubic area after you're invaded."

CHAPTER 11
Social Pestilence

Every other year medical science finds a new social disease that scares the wits out of us. Unfortunately, they don't find the cures as quickly as they find the disease. The Bible thumpers tell us that these afflictions appear as a punishment for the promiscuous and a hurdle for stopping would-be sinners before they start. They might be right, but from my observations, it's stopping nothing. The media exploits our fears by presenting half-hour specials or lengthy features dealing with the latest hurdle. For a change, the media now helps us with some in-depth education.

We face today a mixed bag of clap, crabs, herpes and AIDS. Avoid these. Nonspecific infections which cause dripping and itching can't be traced directly to fooling around because they *are* nonspecific. They lack a name, and most people don't pay definite attention when things remain unnamed. Herpes and AIDS, however, seem to be the main topic of discussion at almost every cocktail party.

All you sinners must spend a day in the medical section at the public library. Volumes of material await. Your best bet? Request the latest research information from the librarian at least twice a year. If you watch television, newscasters will report any new breakthrough.

This book is not a medical text but you might find these facts helpful. Venereal disease, although not given the media space it deserves, still rages in pandemic proportions. It's unavoidable unless the man uses condoms. Yes, you may find it a bit awkward rushing to your first breathless meeting with Hal carrying a three-pack of pink-ribbed condoms in your purse. Did you know condoms now come in a variety of pastel shades and textures? Designer condoms (what will they think of next?). If the gentleman is married, he might consider wearing the formfitting raincoat. Raincoat is a locker room term commonly used by men. If he's single, he may react adversely, insulted by your fears of disease. How dare you accuse him of being dirty. Of course, he answers to no one if he becomes infected except the Health Department.

The married gentleman cohabits most nights with a wife who doesn't cheat (*sure* he does), and can't risk infecting her. I know a promiscuous doctor, highly paranoid, who would not consider going at it without his condoms. Doctors see so much havoc in families after the person who does not cheat catches VD from the spouse who does. Do not hesitate giving one of those pink jobs to a medical man you're enjoying an affair with. He'll compliment your awareness.

Some women never know they have VD. There are symptoms in the acute stage that pass rather quickly in the chronic stage. You might experience burning when urinating, or a discharge. If you know your husband cheats, neither of you will know who introduced it. If he discovers his infection first, he will feign outrage, never admitting that he caught it outside the home. Don't get trapped into a confession. Even if he is faithful, admit nothing. You proclaim greater surprise and outrage than he. If you undergo grilling for days, don't crack. It's impossible detecting who caught it first. Nothing can ever be positively proven without a confession. He might suspect but, great actress that you are, you know nothing. A friend once told me that the best defense is an offense. So, even if you know you are the giver, attack him for infecting you. Amid the confusion and commotion, the entire issue, with no answers, should die down as soon as the doctor administers the penicillin and you both recover.

A young married woman I knew some years ago told me about her doctor's appointment that week. She praised her husband with such tender adoration because he had made the appointment. It seems he had caught some kind of bug and, protecting her to the max, didn't want her catching it. "The doctor will inject you with a serum of some sort that will prevent you from getting sick," he said. With my general knowledge of medicine, this sounded fishy. But I said nothing and forgot about it until I heard the local gossipmonger tell everyone she could get her claws on that her husband knew the doctor who had given my friend a penicillin shot. Her husband had the clap; the doctor agreed to tell her nothing except the fishy story, and treat her accordingly. Very unethical, but it worked. Remember the fraternity of men I spoke about in an earlier chapter? I don't consider this duped lady stupid. She knew nothing about medicine and trusted her husband. He was in the doghouse either way if she discovered the plot. He knew she was clean and took his chances with the lie. If any of you ladies know a doctor who will duplicate this deed and a husband you know will not question the shots, go for it. If not, and you discover the infection, storm home screaming like hell, stare him down with murderous accusations and live through the month of mayhem. If he's dillied or dallied with someone else, he might just take the blame.

Crabs, those dreadful little creatures, crawl around your pubic area after you're invaded. You can't miss them. You eventually will see them in abundance, and they itch. But unless you use a high-intensity flashlight, inspecting every man you're with, you won't discover the affliction until after they multiply in your pubic area. Some men can transfer the critters before they know they're carriers themselves. In any case, let's assume you're it. "I got them from a toilet seat at Saks," is your story. "You know I never sit down, but that one time I just forgot. I'm going to sue the store." He won't let you. Even though the sitting transmission is rare, cling to it for dear life. If you experience a crab clan and haven't had intercourse with your husband, you still must admit this particular curse. Clothing and bedding must be treated, as well as your body. Inform the man who shares your marriage bed of the problem so he can treat himself as well. If not eradicated, you can trade them back and forth forever. So own up to the little critters, curse the rotten toilet seat repeatedly, and start shampooing. If you're really devious, wait until your husband starts scratching and blame his rotten toilet seat. We all must act in the manner that makes us most comfortable.

Herpes is a bit more serious. To date there is no known cure for it. We see lots of people with cold sores on their lips. This form of herpes is transmittable but not the same form associated with sex. I would certainly avoid kissing someone with a cold sore. Fortunately, they are visible on the face. Genital herpes is another matter. There are two reasons that genital herpes rages out of control. Infected people keep it a secret, including the woman who conceals the disease between her legs, virtually undetectable to the poor guy who sleeps with her. Many fine people will warn prospective bed partners about their condition, thereby giving the consenting adults a choice. Herpes is contagious when it's active. In its dormant stage it's usually harmless, with some exceptions. Women certainly have the advantage in detection. During foreplay, inspect his genital area. You don't have to be obvious. Stroke his penis. If you detect rough areas that suggest healed scabs, call time out for a discussion. An open sore needs no discussion; it speaks for itself. A healed scab might be something you want to look at. Some penises feel rough in places, but a healed sore is obvious to the naked eye. Even if he's in the dormant stage, don't take the risk. With your husband you'd regulate your intercourse to correspond with his condition. With your lover, unless you plan on spending the rest of your life with him, take the prudent course; make some excuse and leave. Even a minor suspicion of herpes would send me racing from the bed. If he didn't tell you beforehand and you find some evidence of the disease during your tactile inspection, simply leave the premises. If it's someone you know won't fly into a rage and become violent, or someone who has become important to you as a person, then discuss the matter. If you've picked up some guy at the local bar and know only that he's adorable and spinning your propellers, you might really tick him off with your suspicion of his damaged organ. Herpes, a very unpleasant fact of life, affects the best and worst of people. It's not dirty or disgraceful. It's simply a disease with no cure as yet. You avoid it by looking before you leap.

We all know about AIDS. Use condoms in all situations. Some of us don't heed this advice and think this disease can never happen to us. Some of us live dangerously and some of us get sick. Enough said.

"Check the bed and couch for underwear discarded haphazardly in the heat of passion."

CHAPTER 12
Affair Etiquette

One can successfully muddle through life without knowing which fork you use for the salad and which one for the entrée. Also, do you serve from the left or from the right? You may even slurp your soup in the finest restaurant without a deafening silence from the other patrons, aghast at your bourgeois table manners. Etiquette for the masses now consists of "doing your own thing." It's nice to know but not crucial to your existence,

The sort of etiquette that follows is crucial to your existence as a married woman and to your image as a successful cheater with style and couth. Why not be the best you can be at everything, including cheating?

When Alexander Graham Bell invented the telephone, how could he know what a lethal weapon he unleashed on the world? Like most great inventions, you can use it for good or evil. I categorize the telephone as the single most important item in a woman's wardrobe. That instrument probably spends more time on our person than any other item purchased in our lifetime. It's indispensable for our jobs as household engineers, mommies, out-of-home employment, social arrangements, gossiping with the girls, and secretive, furtive, often monosyllabic conversations with lovers.

You know how it goes. He calls you at home while you're peeling potatoes. It's family time, everyone's at home, and with three phone extensions in rooms you have no visual access to, you speak like a badly trained Russian spy in a James Bond flick. "Yes, no, of course, yes, yes, 'bye." Anyone could be listening to his conversation on the extensions. Your family knows that you never limited yourself to six words in any conversation in your life, especially on the phone. You attract more attention by being almost wordless than by speaking normally. Of course, with Hal you can't speak normally. In your home Hal doesn't exist. Some women play cryptic games on the phone. They pretend it's a familiar friend, using her name, and discuss a luncheon or dinner date. That is a dangerous ploy if your female friend knows nothing of the deception, and if she does know, it's even more dangerous.

We also recall the whisperers. These ladies carry on short "psst, psst" conversations with Hal, usually retreating into a corner of the kitchen, hunched over the mouthpiece looking quite nervous and guilty. Secrets create a body language all their own. "Who was that, honey?" hubby asks.

"Oh, that was just Gloria calling about the PTA meeting."

Unless you actually are a secret agent, that kind of sophomoric performance on more than one occasion will trigger the beginning of suspicion.

As a business woman, always on call with the phone ringing off the hook most of the time, you can make the date out loud. Who'll know it isn't business? But why do that? The woman who parades her affair before her family, enjoying her deception and the intrigue of it all, is asking for trouble.

There is only one Double-O Seven, and he is fictional.

Your family soon will regard hang-ups and wrong numbers a nuisance and become suspicious when they happen frequently. An old burlesque joke, "If a man answers, hang up," may make you the target of a pie in the kisser.

Phoning you at home is in bad taste, ergo, poor etiquette. You must show respect for your family and for yourself. He knows you're executing some fancy footwork keeping the affair alive, but he need not see it. Request the right to do the communicating. It may put some strain on his privacy, but you'll find ways of easing that problem.

He should not be privy to your family life unless you so choose. When you receive his calls at home, he becomes aware of your disrespect for your family. It doesn't do a lot for your image. If you retain your ladylike demeanor with Hal, he becomes fully aware that you are not only a respectful person but also clever. With no phone proof on your end, he becomes a safer affair. For the most part, Hal will follow your lead, less likely to make careless errors if you don't. He will think more of you as a person if he sees how considerately you treat others, and safer knowing you are a master at covering your tracks. He doesn't like the idea of getting caught any more than you do. You have a great deal to lose; if not a great deal, at least something worth preserving for the present. Always make him aware of that.

If Hal is married, he deserves the same etiquette. If he's too dense, too busy or too rude, you must set the example and educate him with some rules and regulations. He may not care if his wife discovers his indelicacy. She may already know about his last ten flings and chooses to live with them. Eleven, however, may be her breaking point, in which case she could shake the tree her lemon hangs on— bringing you down with it. You shake it first and dislodge the rotten fruit. Climbing this tree could be hazardous to your health.

If your man is married and plans on staying that way, execute meeting arrangements without calls at either residence. Spontaneity is a state of being neither of you will enjoy often. On the rare occasion it does occur, you will savor it that much more. You can make your next date after each meeting. If one of you fails to show, the other cannot ease his or her mind about a possible pileup on the freeway by phoning the house. The missing party may sneak away and make a quick call, but if this poses a risk, no recriminations should be forthcoming.

Ideally, he runs or works for a business, and a private phone line makes things so much the better. If not, put into action a plan discussed and mutually agreed upon by both of you. Fooling a smart secretary is not always easy. You can play the part of a customer or client, using a prearranged name. If he doesn't accept your call, there's a reason, so don't try again for a while. If you feel like investing some gray matter into this deception, he can invent his own code so you will know when to call back. For example, "busy" means not today, "lunch" or "dinner" means call back soon. If you're going through the same secretary each time, she will start recognizing your voice. Don't get too chummy with her; keep it businesslike and always use the same name, definitely not your own.

If you can predict your husband's estimated time of arrival and leaving as regularly as the sun rising and setting, allowing infrequent calls at home in cases of dire emergencies is okay. Always, one call will come when hubby is home with the sniffles. This can trip you up. When a woman talks with a man she loves to fondle, something glorious happens. This radiance proves difficult to conceal from the man she lives with. Cell phones rule for cheating, so figure out a way to introduce one if you don't have one already.

I know this sounds clinical and devoid of romance. It's better than being devoid of credit cards or possibly your limbs, which might occur if you glow like a nuclear reactor on the phone, ostensibly with the Maytag repairman in the form of Hal.

As the affair blossoms and you become more familiar, consider verbal etiquette a must. Forgo prying into his personal life. It's tacky. Ditto for depicting your spouse as a composite moron and fiend. Talk about what the man you're in bed with finds relative. If he believes you should know that his wife sells her body to the highest bidder or the grocery boy, he'll tell you. If he does, make no judgments. He can say what he likes; he won't appreciate it, though, if you agree and jointly condemn the lady. He may not think badly of you at the moment, but the first time she commits a saintly deed, he may remember your judgment.

He moans about her constantly and you start expecting his disappointments. You arrive at your meeting place. Trying to console his wounded libido, you promptly ask, "How is the slut this week?" She, however, has just saved one of the kids from drowning in the neighbor's pool. It won't make for a pleasant afternoon. If you continuously paint your husband in shades of black, you create a depressing aura. Your lover seeks escape from unpleasant details, just like you. If you both bring your messy trash into the new bed, you escape nothing. It's tacky. You might as well stay at home with Herbie, clod that he may be.

The same holds true for the kids. Who among us has perfect kids? Discuss their triumphs. Keep the conversation as positive as you can, avoiding talk of prison sentences and terminal truancy.

Discussing former playmates, unless used as an erotic fantasy in bed, will produce many negative reactions. Let him think he's the second. No one ever believes he's the first, even if he is. If he thinks you've entertained a platoon or a regiment, the last hurrah is in sight. You may give the best head in the world and orgasm for real. You may be the best lady he's ever met, but you also represent a hotbed of disease and scuz. It's that double standard again. It's also his ego.

If you cheat with one man or half the world, make each one believe he is your only action. "Gee, Hal, I can't see you today. I have another date," is okay in the single world. Affairs run differently. Marital infidelity stands as a world unto itself. Playing with one toy while your permanent toy remains at home is all the action you need. Married ladies aren't supposed to cheat. Fact of life. Married men are. Fact of life. If you dally only with Hal, Hal will create in his mind a valid reason for your infidelity. He must so he can feel good about himself, not for Freddie and Stanley. If he's screwing your brains out, it must be right. He can't justify your infidelity to him. It sounds crazy but from my experience and observation, it's right on. You can begin the affair with all sorts of plans for uninvolved, free actions, but we never achieve freedom from one another, particularly those we sleep with.

Household etiquette covers a broad spectrum. In all of these categories, if you are observant you will begin seeing the connection between good manners and personal safety. Doing the "right" thing often is the safe thing to do.

Cleaning ranks high on the list of loathsome tasks. During the early years of my marriage, I sprang out of bed at dawn, mop in hand, addressing the toilet and surrounding areas of my home with eager enthusiasm. This was my Camelot, and it would sparkle for my Lancelot. That lasted about two years. Lance hardly noticed my efforts and usually missed the bowl, making my task difficult and unappreciated. I worked an eight-hour day before the children arrived, as he did. Soon it became my privilege to watch my prince relax his royal bones in front of the TV as I began the night shift. Fortunately, a large family room accommodated my ironing board. I timed the pressing to coincide with the "Movie of the Week." What a lucky girl.

After the children came in rapid succession, my home resembled a badly fought war. No truces, no peace talks. No respite. There's nothing new here, ladies. Robert Young didn't live in my house. "Father Knows Best" aired as a fantasy I thought my neighbors experienced. After meeting all my neighbors, I accepted it for what it was—a chauvinistic, propagandist lie put on by an all-male network, tranquilizing the housewives lest they eventually discover their rights and stage a subsequent uprising.

When you clean Hal's house, look upon it in a different light. You must also clean Hal's house well. Every evidence of your presence must disappear before you do. Check the bed and couch for underwear discarded haphazardly in the heat of passion. Check the bathroom for makeup, the living room for gloves or scarves, and the kitchen for keys or your wallet. Please don't conduct this treasure hunt like Sherlock Holmes stalking Professor Moriarty.

You've just enjoyed a lovely time, so keep the mood appropriately light and charming. Being the marvelous creature Hal knows you are, you insist on tidying up. He insists on doing it himself. He has a maid coming in the morning. You wouldn't hear of it as you straighten the sheets. Keep in mind, this is not your husband. Your lover will honor your silly little whims if you insist in a cute, feminine manner. Wrinkle your nose with a purry "Please," and he'll probably surprise you with a set of monogrammed cleaning utensils the next time you rendezvous.

You don't know if you will ever see that house again. You don't know who will see it next. Who knows? The little devil may be doing the other three members of your tennis foursome. Leave no clues.

If you occupy a hotel or, God forbid, a motel, execute the same caution. Let him leave first; he might think you a bit odd with this compulsion of cleaning public places. Be a thorough investigator. If you leave something, like a wallet, that's traceable directly to you, they will contact your home. Just your luck, finding the only honest innkeeper in your county on the day of your finest and hottest transgression. It could put a damper on the memory.

Under no circumstances should passion lead both your bodies to your bed. This kind of behavior goes beyond bad manners. It's suicidal. A friend, whose husband was a major league ballplayer, would jump into her sack, turn the radio dial to her husband's game, then fun and frolic until the seventh inning stretch, if it was a home game. Road games gave her an extra two innings. As long as she heard his name in the lineup, the lovers went stroke for stroke without missing a beat. Even with the odds in her favor, I still thought it a poor choice of locations. Other people might witness his entering and exciting. A visiting friend or relative spelled danger. You can always find alternate choices other than your home; if not, find an alternate man.

Always inspect automobiles, those handy scenes of foreplay and sometime conclusions, after you realign your pretzeled limbs and before you kiss good night. Small articles slip into crevices, remain there for weeks, then surface in the lascivious vehicle on the way to your mother-in-law's Sunday dinner with the family. If it's a really lousy karma day, your mother-in-law may be the lucky one who finds the pink-ribbed condom in the back seat.

We've covered his house, hotels and motels, and both cars. Stay away from your house, but if you tempt fate, be extra careful. Exercise extreme caution, trying not to lose things in places clearly off limits. If you're not a frequent lounge lizard, clutch your personal possessions when you meet for cocktails twenty miles from home.

Thus you can avoid spending three days explaining your sudden thirst for gin after spending two days explaining your sudden urge to explore a part of town you previously detested and wouldn't be caught dead in. If caught in circumstances like these, shrug them off as another symptom of your impending menopause and mid-life crisis. If he keeps harping on your strange and suspicious behavior, make another doctor's appointment, again exhibiting erratic and wacky behavior. As your medical bills climb steadily upward, watch his harping diminish on an almost equal curve. Your doctor unwittingly becomes your finest ally. God bless the medical man and his endless quests in the form of endless tests with endless expense.

"If your spouse captures you and Hal stark naked in his marble tub full of bubbles, don't plead guilty."

CHAPTER 13
Deny Everything

In the event your spouse captures you and holds you prisoner after finding you with Hal, stark naked in his marble tub filled with bubbles, you will not honor his accusations by pleading guilty. This is not the time or place for any sort of discussion. While those around you become highly emotional, you remain calm and immediately take control. Hal trembles, Herbie rages, and you are equally insulted and angry at their threats, bad language and childish behavior. You deserve to be treated like the lady you are. Unless your husband murders people with axes, you need not fear for Harold's safety. Both of them, taken aback by your presentation, will postpone the pending ugly scene until you separate Herbie from what he has just seen. If you do it quickly, you may successfully modify the truth a bit and make Herbie believe that what he actually saw varies somewhat from what he thinks he saw. You can execute this invaluable kind of diversionary move in many ways.

You will not become part of the confusion if you act like the outraged party and throw them a curve, causing confusion in another area. You, in effect, yell "Fire!" when there's a flood. Change the visual scene as quickly as possible. Don't become a still life, allowing your husband time for mental notes of position, place, or state of undress. If he catches you in a bed, move quickly out of it and into another room.

Leave the premises alone and in haste. Don't go home; he needs cooling-down time. He needs time for all sorts of doubts and fears to soften while alone and contemplating. A quick discussion at the scene is not in your best interests. Your attitude during the aftermath sets the stage for your eventual victory or defeat. If you crack up, whimpering apologies and excuses, consider your fate sealed. Please, always remember psychology. Your husband will treat you in a manner corresponding to the way you present yourself. I am not saying that he will exonerate you and give you the medal of honor, but you will at least buy some time so you and your husband can discuss your problem with dignity. Catching you in the sack does not entitle him to mistreat you physically or emotionally.

In a few rare instances women caught sharing their passion actually made their husbands believe the entire incident was not what it seemed. This happens maybe once every million times. The goal: A plan of action, taken in well designed steps, that keeps you home, assuming that's the location you prefer, without undergoing torture and being driven crazy. Follow these steps:

1. Remain calm and admit nothing. In fact, saying nothing would be the ideal during the actual capture. Keep yourself composed and well-bred with a decidedly innocent stance.

2. Give your husband time for venting his anger on something other than your person.

3. Set up a meeting in a neutral zone, still retaining your poise, no matter what he says, and shoot for that one-in-a-million chance. He might be that rare bird who believes

you plopped in that tub for business reasons, blackmail or charity. It depends on how he sees you as a person. If you absolutely must save the world, he might listen as you describe your attempt to keep Hal from taking his life because of some newly transpired tragedy he couldn't deal with. By being there, showing him he was still a man, you prevented him from slitting his wrists. Yes, you committed adultery, but at least your motives were pure.

Ideally, in this meeting you would tell him the truth about your reasons for being in that tub. His abuse or lack of attention. Your loneliness and confusion. Possibly your fear of aging, or even discussing all your fears about life and what's in your heart. I believe that any man who understood your actions and offered you assistance in dealing with the fears and concerns that caused the present problem would qualify as a man you wouldn't cheat on in the first place.

Back to reality.

Some clever men and women lull you into a false sense of security. They seem understanding and interested in knowing everything. He assures you, "No reprisals no matter what you divulge." As soon as you spill your guts, however, Jekyll becomes Hyde and you become the victim. There's no way of knowing this in advance. Your husband, wounded and in pain, can come at you in many different ways.

For instance, he completely breaks down and seeks comfort from you. His pitiful condition appears quite real for the time being. "Tell me how I failed," he pleads, an unstable man for the moment. Give him comfort but withhold information. You are still innocent and will remain so until your death. Otherwise, after he recovers from shock, he can chase you up a tree like a crazed grizzly bear spouting your confession verbatim. He is not clever, just confused. People who hurt want to strike out. Not all of us strike immediately.

Or he's the seemingly violent type, threatening castration and beheading right now. His eyes roll around like cherries in a slot machine, and his tone sounds ominous. The six o'clock news stories about mass murders in families that house adulterers are very rare, considering the population. Thousands of people get caught weekly and few physical catastrophes follow. Verbalizing murder is one thing. Committing it is another. Don't let him scare a confession out of you. If any punching occurs, it will probably be by the two men. Even that is uncommon. Most people abhor pain and are cowards.

Another possibility: He fills you with guilt. "Think of all I've done for you, and how the kids will suffer when they discover their mother's slutty behavior," he says. "Do I deserve this? Would I treat you this way?" Along with the guilt will come shame. This puts you in a weak position if you allow it to continue. You are, after all, only human and you know society condemns your adultery. Don't tune out this whining unless you possess a strong sense of yourself. Guilt and shame make psychiatrists wealthy. We all feel some. Don't fall into a black well of despair and fill yourself with guilty recriminations. You have not committed a major crime.

I know husbands, perpetrators of many infidelities their wives never knew about, who became the most outraged about their wives' peccadilloes. They stir a strange mix of their own guilt with a badly wounded ego. They remember how much they enjoyed cheating and, projecting their remembrance on the unfaithful wife, they become impossible. Those professional cheaters of long standing will project that as well. If it's your first time, they will imagine you tootling the Marine marching band and scrimmaging with all of the National Football League for the last fifteen years. These are difficult people to reason with.

Let's say he didn't actually see you, but he catches you in an incriminating lie. Your surprise at his interrogation is the first cop-out. "Am I a child who must answer for my every move?" you ask indignantly. Keep asking these questions while he's throwing you his. Answer his question with another question until you think of a reasonable answer. Finally, give him this answer with reluctance and hurt. Don't talk to him for a couple of days. It may discourage him from approaching you this way again.

All this sounds cold and callous. Let me tell you, ladies, that men have been using this information for centuries. I spoke to many men before and during the writing of this book. Most of them laughed and thought the premise comical. Some called it stupid, and not one took it seriously. That attitude allows them to boast of their brilliance in sidestepping questioning wives. Some had the effrontery to recount tales of wives catching them in their family beds with "chicks" and they told their spouses they were seeing nothing. The girls were figments of their overwrought imaginations. They kept brainwashing until the wives almost believed their insanity. The men used the offensive role to the hilt, nagging and bedeviling until their wives were so worn down it wasn't possible to continue. The wives' questions weren't worth the verbal punishment that followed. I am again not passing judgment, only reporting what I have learned over the years.

Cheating is a national epidemic. It may cause pain. If you can do it successfully without causing pain, so much the better. With or without this book, cheating will go on as long as marriage exists. For every action there is a reaction. Keep a low profile. You are not a second class citizen any more. Men do not have the market cornered on cheating. You deserve as much information as they have. Equality between the sexes should extend into the strange bedroom in the form of education as well as performance.

Good luck.

P.S. You may as well have some fun to go with your luck.

"You are still innocent and will remain so until your death."

About the author

With or Without Roller Skates, a black comedy about my life as a physical therapist, is a book I co-authored. Paramount and Lorimar optioned it specifically for Barbra Streisand. I wrote a movie entitled "Going Back" and a television pilot about the garment industry. My other credits include articles published in Gambling Times, Poker Player and Back in the Bronx magazines.

My second husband and I lived in Bel Air, Malibu and Palm Desert in the 70's when flower power, wife swapping and swinging were all the rage. Sex, drugs and rock and roll were the order of the day. Our table at the Polo Lounge, nights at the Daisy, Fireside Inn (swing heaven) and friends' homes produced fodder for my research. We spent the '80s in Malibu, San Francisco and New York, where matrimonial ruses seemed non-existent and the gloves were definitely off.

I barely survived women's lib, but did enjoy the bonding and sharing of information that continued on into the new millennium among women of all ages. Men had no idea what we were doing. We had no idea what were doing, and couldn't foresee the confusion and havoc thrust upon the male population. The bollixed-up condition continues to this day, causing horrific problems between the sexes and cheating that is approaching epidemic proportions.

The majority of women I interviewed for this book lacked a clue about having an affair without giving up their lives. Many of them had already diddled about, barely scraping through the experience in one piece. They wondered how men had cornered the market on infidelity so successfully. The men's club, so to speak, became an object of desire by women.

The '90s, '00 and '01 found us getting older but not smarter. I traveled the country, stopping in the Midwest, south and all points east and west. Women had better jobs, making more money with very grand titles, and were even more restless and frustrated than their mamas and aunties had been in the '60s. Why did we burn our brassieres, I wonder?

Printed in the United States
29579LVS00015B/7

9 781418 453480